An Intelligent Person's Guide
to Judaism

An Intelligent Person's Guide to Judaism

SHMULEY BOTEACH

Duckworth Overlook
London · New York · Woodstock

First published in the United States in 2005 by
Duckworth Overlook

LONDON:
Gerald Duckworth & Co. Ltd.
90-93 Cowcross Street
London EC1M 6BF
inquiries@duckworth-publishers.co.uk
www.ducknet.co.uk

NEW YORK:
The Overlook Press
141 Wooster Street
New York, NY 10012

WOODSTOCK:
The Overlook Press
One Overlook Drive
Woodstock, NY 12498
www.overlookpress.com
[For individual orders, bulk and special sales, contact our Woodstock office]

Cataloging-in-Publication Data is available from the
Library of Congress and the British Library

Typeset by Ray Davies
Manufactured in the United States of America
3 5 7 9 8 6 4 2
ISBN-10 1-58567-808-2   ISBN-13 978-1-58567-808-2
ISBN-10 0-7156-3190-X (UK)   ISBN-13 978-0-7156-3190-4 (UK)

Contents

For
Barbara and Stanley, Adrianne and Clive,
Sue and Leo, Fiona and Gary, Teddie,
Penny and Michael, Judy and Harry,
Betty and Cyril, Sarah and Robert,
and Adelene

Acknowledgements

It has always been my dream to write a book about Judaism but I have refrained from doing so for fear that it would be inadequate. While I am not one of its exemplary sons, my Jewish faith has always been my greatest love and inspiration. Knowing that, throughout history, millions of Jews have laid down their lives for the sake of their Judaism rather than relinquish the faith of their ancestors has given me considerable pause in undertaking this task. In the end it was entirely due to the encouragement of Robin Baird-Smith, my publisher and friend, that this book was written at all, and it is he who must take credit for it. So here you have a book on Judaism inspired by a Roman Catholic. I would also particularly like to thank Martin Rynja, my editor at Duckworth.

The book is an attempt to offer traditional Judaism to a modern audience in a rational, intelligible, and engaging light. It incorporates the insights of many great Jewish thinkers. Many thoughts, for example, belong to the old giants of Jewish history, such as Maimonides, but there is also much included from more contemporary Jewish thinkers. Foremost on this list are my teacher and mentor, the Lubavitcher Rebbe, Rabbi Menachem Mendel Schneerson, Rabbi Samson Raphael Hirsch, Rabbi Joseph Dov Soloveitchik, and Rabbi Abraham Joshua Heschel. Other scholars whose luminous ideas I have incorporated include Rabbi Dr Norman

Lamm, Dennis Prager, as well as the illustrious Chief Rabbi of Great Britain, Dr Jonathan Sacks.

There are many books written on Judaism, but this one differs in that it seeks to present the ideas behind the Jewish faith in today's context, rather than serve only as a how-to guide to Jewish ritual. Whereas other books present Jewish ideas as having evolved historically, I am seeking to promote the idea that the Jewish religion is a holistic set of inextricably linked values which together comprise a state of the art system for human potential. That Judaism is not seen in this light, but often as a rather arcane and obsolete ritual, accounts for its sad and unjust decline. This book seeks to set the record straight.

The book is also unlike others in that it attempts to demonstrate the relevance of the world's oldest monotheistic faith to men and women of all colours and persuasions. It was not written, nor was it intended, primarily for a Jewish audience. The L'Chaim Society, an educational outreach organisation with branches in Oxford, London, and Cambridge, of which I am a director and founder, is one of the few Jewish organisations in the world that has a high proportion of non-Jewish members. Every Friday night in Oxford, of the hundred or so students who join us for the weekly Friday night Sabbath meal, about thirty or more are non-Jews. They come to L'Chaim not to convert to Judaism, and indeed only a handful of students have converted in the eleven years that I have been in Oxford. Rather, they come because they want a spiritual framework which is about the celebration of life, which glories in human warmth, and which teaches that God is loving, forgiving, and approachable. They wish to enter a religious environment wherein they can laugh and simply be themselves.

In my other books I have thanked my wife Debbie for always being my greatest pillar of support, without which none of my projects would achieve fruition. In this book I thank her not for supporting me, but for inspiring me. Judaism has long maintained that women possess a higher innate spirituality than men. My wife demonstrates this with her absolute love and devotion to Judaism. There is nothing which Judaism requires which is ever a burden to her, and there is nothing it demands in which she does not perceive an immediate inner beauty. It is my great hope that in these pages you too will find some of the life, dynamism, and vibrancy that are Judaism.

As always, I thank Almighty God for granting me the strength to complete this task. I can only hope that I have done His great law a measure of justice.

Rabbi Shmuley Boteach
Tishrei 5759
September, 1998
Oxford, England

Judaism

A State of the Art Programme
for Human Potential

There is something that the Jews and the British have in common. They are both phenomenal inventors but lousy entrepreneurs. Since moving to Britain eleven years ago, I have read countless articles lamenting the fact that British inventors repeatedly come up with remarkable innovations, only to see their ideas developed and marketed in the United States, where venture capital is more readily available. Take that problem, multiply it a thousand-fold, and you have the history of the Jews.

In thinking of golden civilisations and of high points in history, the average person immediately conjures up images of pontificating Greek philosophers, Roman legions shimmering in the dazzling sun, and the artistic wonders of the Renaissance masters. Tell him that in terms of world ideas the Jews have equalled, at times surpassed all these civilisations, and he will break into a fit of giggles. The Jews ... the Jews, he thinks to himself, their place in history ... Ah yes, they're the ones who have served as the world's perennial victims. Aren't they the nation who were defeated by the Romans, slaughtered by the Crusaders, kicked out by the medieval English, expelled by the Spaniards, disembowelled by Chemielnitzky in the Ukraine, massacred by the Russians and the Poles, and then cremated by the Nazis?

Young Jews share this ignorance as much as anyone else. For the eleven years that I have served as director of L'Chaim, we have tried to involve young Jews in Oxford, London and Cambridge in Judaism. Our ultimate purpose is to instil within them a Jewish identity and we have had, thank God, a measure of success, building the society into one of the largest student societies in the university's history. But we have had to do it with a little help from our friends. Mikhail Gorbachev, Diego Maradona, Boy George, Stephen Hawking, Shimon Peres, Binyamin Netanyahu, Bob Hawke, Yitzchak Shamir, Jon Voight, and Leonard Nimoy have all served to pull students through the front door. Why celebrities? Because Judaism today is known among the young for its ritual rather than for its inspiration. Far from its true essence of revolutionary ideas, to them its image is one of decay, a diminishing population, a religion too encumbered by the weight of its own law to make the earth shake for its young. Thinking mistakenly that Judaism has not had any social impact to speak of, they are unaware that by abandoning it they are relinquishing something that should be precious to them.

Yet if we look back, the contribution made by Judaism to world history is enormous. Judaism provided the very cornerstones of civilisation. The Jews gave the world the idea of the one God. To many people today, the name Jesus Christ is far more recognisable. In the Hebrew Bible one finds the concept that all men are created equal in God's image. Today it is called democracy. The idea of a brotherhood of nations and of peace was first mooted in the books of Isaiah and Jeremiah. Now it goes by the name United Nations. 'One must love one's fellow man as oneself' (Leviticus 19:18) was restyled the Golden Rule, and its origin is now perceived as being Jesus's sermon on the mount. Life must be dedicated to the pursuit of justice, goodness, and ethics, or so Judaism says. Today it is known as secular humanism. The Jewish contribution to world history is undisputed. As the journalist and historian Paul Johnson puts it in his *History of the Jews*: 'Without the Jews the world might have been a much emptier place.'

It is ironic, therefore, that the non-Jewish world's perception of the Jews is as a nation of great businessmen. The Jews have given away their wares to every other people for no gain or profit, to the extent that none ever associate the word Jews with their contribution to society. Judaism today isn't even a force shaping the public debate. It has been completely superseded by its daughter religions Christianity and Islam.

Indeed, in an even greater irony of history, it seems that only anti-Semites are excited enough by Judaism to give it its due. In 1899, H.S. Chamberlain published *Foundations of the Nineteenth Century*, a highly anti-Semitic work which was extremely well-received by intellectuals of the day. The London *Times Literary Supplement* called it, 'unquestionably one of the books that really matter.' Chamberlain writes in this book, 'I cannot help shuddering … at the portentous, irremediable mistake the world made in accepting the traditions of this wretched little nation … as the basis of its belief.' He saw a fundamental breakdown in freedom. 'The Jew came into our gay world and spoiled everything with his ominous concept of sin, his law, and his cross.'

This perceived decay was also the core argument of Nietzsche's hatred against Christianity. He asserted that the Jews had played a big joke on the world in the form of the Christian. They had taken strong German Teutonic knights and corrupted them with compassion, forbearance, humility, and prayer. In essence, Judaism had turned them into wimps.

The arch anti-Semite Richard Wagner – H.S. Chamberlain's father-in-law – thus called for a new German religion with no Jewish or Christian influence, clamouring: 'Emancipation from the yoke of Judaism appears to us the foremost necessity'!

What about Judaism Today?

If Jewish ideas today come with the name Christianity, Islam, secular humanism, communism, utopianism, democracy, new-ageism, and even atheism and agnosticism, it must make sense to have a closer look at these ideas to understand modern life.

In fact, I believe that by tracing religion and morality to their biblical origins, we may well be able to learn to understand not just the Jews and Judaism, but our innate need for humanity itself.

Why is Judaism uniquely empowered to offer us these insights into our world and ourselves? Why not one of those modern hot religions? What relevance could Judaism possibly have to the non-Jews who are part of a different faith tradition?

The answer is that our generation seems to lack a particular type of sustenance. A man brings some material to a tailor and asks him to make a pair of trousers. When he comes back a week later, they are not ready. Two weeks later, they still aren't ready. Finally, after six weeks, the trousers are ready. The man tries them on. They fit perfectly. Nonetheless, when it comes time to pay, he can't resist a jibe at the tailor. 'You know,' he says, 'it took God only six days to make the world. And it took you six weeks to make just one pair of trousers.' 'Ah!' the tailor says. 'But look at this pair of trousers, and look at the world.' Today, spiritualist and new-age books top the world's best-seller lists and gurus of every denomination are sought out by young Western minds who are looking for an alternative to a suffocating materialism. But none of these fast-food solutions seem to offer answers with a lasting power beyond the final page.

Don't get me wrong. I am not saying that dark storm clouds are piling up over us and that we should fear the future. The world at large – the macrocosm – is doing quite well today. Certainly it could be better. But it is almost unimaginable that a global conflict, like a third world war, could break out today. There is a sense of peace around us and about our time, in spite of the many regional conflicts. Wealthy countries operate highly developed foreign-aid programmes for the benefit of poorer ones, and among world leaders there seems a genuine desire to police international tension and create stability.

But while this macrocosm improves, the microcosm, the inner world of man, deteriorates with alarming rapidity. As the first generation in human history to be presented with profound challenges about what to do with our lives, we no longer need to work eighteen-hour days just to put bread on the table. What we require is the answer how to master our lives in a confusing world of endless possibility and choice. We want a creed that will offer *us* a life worth living. Instead, thirty years after the sexual revolution, divorce rates are still continuing to rise. Children today shoot at each other with guns. Drug and substance abuse climb with no end in sight, and new anti-depressants like Prozac are treated as miracle drugs. No less than one in four Americans have been treated at some point in their lives for depression, and people watch endless hours of television to while away their time. It seems that for a great many people modern life can be summed up as the endless pursuit of distractions.

Against this emptiness, I believe Judaism provides an answer. Robbed of temporal power ever since the destruction of the first Temple by the Babylonians in 586 BC, Judaism has always concerned itself with the smallest questions of human existence: whom to marry, how to be a good son and honour one's parents, how to practise honesty in business, how to wrestle with and ultimately conquer one's nature, how to refrain from gossiping behind a friend's back, and how to overcome feelings of jealousy and enjoy the good things which happen to colleagues. As a consequence no faith has emphasised the need to *celebrate life* more. Turning their creative powers inwards, the Jews focused them entirely on perfecting life in the world around them. And in well over two thousand years this inversion of effort has wrought huge benefits in the area of human and communal development and closing the generation gap.

Feminine Energy

Judaism's optimism and strength spring from one core idea, the triumph of feminine-passive over masculine-aggressive values. Though often mistaken for a male-oriented religion, Judaism believes man's sensitivity to the reality around him cannot come about until he harnesses his inner feminine energy. Only the reduction of aggression and competitiveness – all of which produce a noise and hindrance preventing man from noticing the truth – can redeem man from his own self-centredness and focus him fully on God and his happiness.

Ultimately, the most respected person in Judaism is the

facilitator, the supreme exponent of the feminine-passive, someone who selflessly puts the welfare of others before him or herself. It is worrying that we are witnessing the complete discrediting of the facilitator in contemporary society. A simple example, a plant or a tree does nothing but service the needs of humans. It oxygenates our planet and ensures that we can survive and breathe. It facilitates and supports our existence. But does that function count with us for anything serious? We require more tangible uses from our environment. That which is not glaringly proactive elicits only a shrug from an indulgent humanity. So we still cut down our rain forests and turn them into paper pulp and furniture. We still mow down orchards and woods to make room for factories and shopping centres.

Likewise, the lowliest profession today is teaching. Miserable salaries are paid and teachers lead what are perceived to be quiet, uneventful lives out of the limelight. But what kind of signal are we beaming out to our children when they see that investment bankers own yachts and racing cars, while school teachers can barely afford to pay their mortgages? Teachers are moulding the minds of our future and we look down upon them. Having lost our appreciation for the facilitator, we don't even value the future of mankind. A more blatant example of the predominance of male self-centredness in our society can hardly be found.

Against this Judaism argues that we need a vision, a plan for long-term goals as an anchor for our existence; man's higher calling is to develop the potential of others. It maintains that, particularly, the fragmentation of the home is in all this one of society's greatest maladies – one which everybody seems to be overlooking. Parents, particularly women, who want to stay at home are castigated for not fulfilling their potential, wasting their education. But being a parent is life's most noble profession. Nurturing a human life is far loftier than selling computers, playing the markets or being a movie star. It is a comment on our time that only proud and accomplished couples are able to overcome the prevailing sentiment.

A Revolutionary Religion

The emphasis on feminine energy may seem straightforward, but in Western history it fashioned a revolution, the first female revolution. And it is important to realise that such revolutionary defiance is typical of Jewish thinking. While Christianity and Islam converted billions, Judaism always remained small yet controversial: always more a voice with something to say. While other religions opted for power, Judaism chose instead influence. When man still only loved his blood relatives and his kinsmen, the Torah given at Mount Sinai struck the first note of opposition. It commanded man to cherish the stranger, the orphan, and the widow and to protect their interests. Peace, it said, is superior to war, forgiveness the master of vengeance. Man must not steal or murder. Blood whether shed on the battlefield or mixed between families is not the supreme motive of our existence. Rape must always be penalised. Marrying a girl against her will must never be allowed. Even sexual laxity must be overcome, in favour of monogamy.

In doing so, the Torah opened up an extraordinary way of thinking. Most importantly, it proclaimed that things are not necessarily the way they ought to be. Might does not make right. Not only the fittest should survive. Everything can, indeed must, be changed and improved. People could upgrade their social station from that of peasant to land-owner. All through personal exertion they could transform themselves from selfish to selfless, from being hoarders to being philanthropic. Merit and study mattered rather than privilege and ancestry. A priestly class rather than a warrior class should inform and lead the nation.

Over time, the Jews have paid a heavy price for bolstering these beliefs in the feminine as many have taken advantage of the vulnerability it engenders. But, significantly, even after this turbulent past the ancient light of Judaism has not dimmed whereas its opponents have faded. No general today is the equal of a winner of the Nobel Peace prize. Indeed, Nobel prize winners are infinitely more regarded than generals. Aspiring conquerors such as Saddam Hussein are seen as nothing more than pathetic and flawed characters. And in the United States a man who eschewed the military, avoided the draft, and even publicly protested against his own country's involvement in a foreign war, has been elected President. Nelson Mandela, someone who would have been dismissed as inconsequential just two generations ago, is now one of the Western world's idols. The same is true of the immensely respected Martin Luther King and Mahatma Ghandi.

That these figures could be so idolised in the Western world today, far more than the 'courageous' terrorists who stake their lives in order to bring about political ends, even appears to point to a triumph of the feminine-passive values of Judeo-Christianity over the masculine-aggressive values of the ancient world. Even in commerce, businessmen are discouraged from thinking in terms of winning and devouring the competition. Contemporary thinking goes that corporate titans must always think 'win-win' rather than 'win-lose'. A deal should be profitable to both parties, a total reversal from the cut-throat commercial practices of just one generation ago, when brutal negotiations and putting the competition out of business were as important as winning new customers.

Today's Revolution

But we would deceive ourselves if we thought the feminine revolution is victorious, or that it can be deemed to be nearing its end. It is simply the battle lines that have been redrawn. Today, of course, the desire to win glory on the battlefield has been largely transmuted to making money in the markets. A former Oxford student who now works at a bank in London told me that he was getting a lot of hassle from his workaholic boss whenever he left work early on Friday in deference to the Jewish Sabbath. 'That's because you challenge him', I said. 'Whenever you leave early, you remind him that there are things in life more important than making money. He then must ask himself why he is still at work rather than being home with his wife and children.'

This example of the Sabbath is perhaps the most powerful illustration of where we find ourselves nowadays. The Jewish mystics explain that the six days of the week represent the masculine-aggressive dimension in creation. They are the time for work, success, and development where everything is governed by considerations of human utility. Conversely, the Sabbath day, which has always been described by the ancient rabbis in feminine terms – the Shabbos Queen, the Shabbos Bride – is a time for rest, nurture, study, tranquillity, and holiness. It is holier than any day of the week when man masters the world.

To go against this sentiment amounts to a denial of one's

own needs and those of society. A mother of the household gathering her children around her in the presence of her husband and lighting the Sabbath candles at sunset on Friday night is one of the most moving moments in Jewish life. It represents the belief that we should strive to be a source of illumination to others, that we were all created not only to be happy ourselves, but to make others happy. Family life is essential for this light to shine and enable us to realise that we should aim not just to succeed ourselves, but to encourage, applaud, and welcome the success of others, not just to feed ourselves, but to feed the stranger even at personal sacrifice.

A Religion of Deeds

At this point you may well ask where this leaves the religious aspect of Judaism? If Judaism has already imparted its wealth of content and meaning to Western society, why not consign its religious message to the dustbin of history? It would seem that all of the above has long been assimilated in European culture, and that it only needs restating every now and then.

There is one very good reason why this would be the wrong approach. Judaic philosophy works; but it works because it is a religion. As it is not just another collection of ideas, picking and choosing would seriously defeat its logic. A religion concerned primarily with realities rather than intangibles, Judaism treats concepts like feminine energy, facilitation and revolutionary thought as no more than tools of convenience. The very purpose of Jewish thought is to take ethereal, spiritual abstractions and translate them into a reality which becomes inseparable from human living. It is precisely its religious message that sensitises man to reality around him. Not only do human beings need a strong belief in values and ideas, we need to make them work for us. Our personal contentment is too firmly rooted in acts rather than their abstractions, and this is what Judaism constantly reminds one of. Not all of us appreciate that both values and ideas are useless unless they are ingrained within the human character. All great ideas, as well as civilisation itself, corrode with time. And, like flowers cut off from their roots, values will slowly wilt and die if left untended. We sometimes forget how easy it is for ethics to go out of fashion, even when, not much over fifty years ago, the Nazis trampled on all of these values and ideas.

It is of great importance that there is a coherent programme of action within which to implement ethics, a belief in deeds that ensures that values take root within the psyche of the individual and each successive generation. And it is precisely the religious side of Judaism that helps us turn our values into deeds. Judaism is a religious programme of action whose purpose it is to connect man with God, thereby making men Godly.

What Makes Judaism Different from Other Religions

Well before Karl Marx dismissed religion as the opiate of the masses, writers attacked religious individuals as people who are in need of a crutch. As H.L. Mencken wrote, 'God is the immemorial refuge of the incompetent, the helpless, the miserable. They find not only sanctuary in His arms, but also a kind of superiority, soothing to their lacerated egos: He will set them above their betters.' Similarly, Francis Picabia wrote, 'Men have always need of god! A god to defend them against other men.'

There is some truth in these criticisms. Religion is a source of strength to the helpless, a source of life to those verging on death, a source of hope to those in despair, and a source of inspiration to the fatigued and disillusioned. The saying goes that there are no atheists in the bomb-shelter.

Indeed, I have no problem admitting that religion is a crutch. Experiencing insecurity is part and parcel of being human. Some gain strength by placing themselves at the centre of an ever-expanding circle of possessions. Others need to control and dominate their peers. Still others try to fill their existential void by sleeping with as many members of the opposite sex as possible.

If it is meaning we all crave, then there can be little harm in choosing something truly meaningful like religion. Any real religion will attempt to go further than a shot of temporary relief. Starting where human limitations end, they afford man the opportunity to enter in a relationship with God and His creation. With this focus on the potential greatness of man, religion ultimately seeks to unlock the vast store of purpose that would otherwise remain trapped within our person.

Man's Relationship with God

As the first purpose of religion is to provide a relationship with God, the question becomes, how can one enjoy a relationship with God? And, preceding that question, how may God be apprehended? All religions pose these questions as their starting point. Of course, every world religion is distinguished from the others by a unique theology and in the details of its observance.

There are two principal ways for man to bridge the chasm separating him from his Creator. First, religion can help man to ascend to the heavens. Such upward-looking theologies have a simple solution to the 'quantum gap' problem: man must renounce his place on earth. Man sleeps, eats, lusts, has sex, pursues gold, and ultimately dies and becomes fodder for worms. But God does or suffers none of these things. Hence, only by forsaking them can man become 'spiritual' and embrace the divine.

On this model, religion serves as ladder: if you do this and don't do that, you will grow closer to the deity. A common thread linking Christianity and the other world religions which are exponents of this approach is their varying degree of asceticism. Man must first divest himself of his peculiarly human limitations. Christianity's holy men commit themselves to poverty, chastity and silence while Islam teaches that the highest fulfilment of religion lies in holy war and dying as a martyr for the spread of one's faith. Hare Krishnas achieve ultimate bliss by becoming wandering mendicants, renouncing all material possessions, while Buddhists seek nirvana through the total expiation of self.

Not surprisingly, the most poignant example of the anti-worldliness of these religions is their attitude toward death. Death is seen as a beneficent release from the cage of an un-Godly body and a corrupt world. It is death, therefore, which brings the ultimate redemption and elevation. In Christianity, churches are surrounded by cemeteries, and relics taken from the bodies of saints serve as the highest spiritual articles within the great cathedrals. Indeed, it was specifically the suffering and death of Christ while in bodily form which brought forth human salvation.

Elevated by this spiritual attention, death itself is by no means straightforward in Christianity, as reflected in the gospel's oft-quoted statement 'It is more difficult for the rich man to enter the kingdom of heaven than it is for a camel to pass through the eye of a needle' (Matth. 19:24). Paraphrasing the thoughts of Rabbi Samson Raphael Hirsch, the essence of Christianity is the feeling of absolute dependence on a Higher Power. Man is shown the bestial forces which overwhelm him and allowed to wish for the higher power that, through 'faith', should save him from their fetters. Aware of the nocturnal spirit of passion and evil in his own breast, he becomes frightened of himself and, in the horror of the night, seeks salvation at the altar of Christ. Thus, Christianity likes to celebrate its holy mysteries preferably at night, and its fervent prayers are a cry of distress from the power of the 'evil' in the world and in one's own heart. Man is tied to the Divine by passiveness.

Heaven on Earth

Judaism is the one world religion that belongs to a uniquely different type. It categorically rejects the belief that God occupies the heavens and shuns a lowly earth. On the contrary, Isaiah declares, 'Holy, holy, holy is the Lord of Hosts; the whole earth is full of his glory' (6:3). To Judaism, a rejection of the physical world would ultimately amount to a rejection of God's omnipresence. As the great medieval Jewish philosopher Rabbi Judah Halevi wrote in his magnum opus, *Kuzari*, 'The servant of God does not withdraw himself from secular contact lest he be a burden to the world and the world to him; he does not hate life, which is one of God's bounties granted to him … On the contrary, he loves this world and a long life'.

The purpose of man from a Jewish perspective is to cause God to dwell here on earth. All of earth's creation has a potential for holiness, irrespective of heaven. Rabbinical legend tells of a dispute in which the angels asked God why He had forsaken them in favour of Abraham. The Almighty responded, 'You angels made Me Master over the heavens, where I have always been King. But Abraham made Me Master over the earth where previously I was unknown.'

If all that exists in the physical world has potential for consecrating the earth, then the charge of man is to reveal that latent holiness through his actions. Man has inherent powers for holiness he must use. There is a Godly way to eat and drink, a Godly way to think and speak, and even a Godly way to make love. The Ten Commandments, given by God, illustrate the majestic scope of his mission on earth. They soar from the most basic 'I am the Lord your God' to embrace the whole gamut of human existence. Even thoughts are included, 'Do not covet your neighbour's wife or possessions'.

The most powerful demonstration of Judaism's embracing of the physical world is the fact that the very symbol of God's covenant with the Jew is the sign of circumcision, placed on the male sexual organ. It is He who created passion in man's breast so that man, with independent power, might master it in the service of God. Thus, the symbol of circumcision lies in the moral sphere. It is an expression of freedom and an affirmation of life, reminding man that he is always capable of transcending the ranks of the animal. But it also represents the capacity of man to use all his powers, even his sensual inclinations, for a free, moral and consecrated life in the service of God.

Judaism is, therefore, no 'religion' in the ordinary sense of the word, but revealed legislation. By charging man to submit of his own free will to the law of God, the law of life, it makes man conscious of both the possibility and power of his free will. What Judaism demands in the service of God is not merely the prayers and litanies of desperadoes, but the complete and joyful, free and happy devotion of man in his rule over the world.

It goes further than that. Man has a right, indeed an obligation, to partake of the bounty of the earth. Pleasure, life, power, freedom, sensuality and happiness are for Judaism the heralds that lead to God. But at the same time that bounty must never obscure the Almighty. Sexual desire is good. When practised in marriage, it is the holiest of human undertakings, capable of sewing together two strangers as one flesh. The pursuit of wealth need be neither selfish nor evil, provided man acts charitably in accordance with God's laws. This most fundamental difference between Judaism and Christianity is expressed by Rabbi Hirsch in the following saying: 'Judaism allows man to find God where man finds himself; whereas Christianity allows man to find God where man loses himself.'

Unmasking the World

If, as Judaism asserts, God is to be found as much on earth as He is in the heavens, the obvious question is, how can so many of us fail to notice him? The truth is that nature conceals Him. The Hebrew word for nature is *tevah*, which also means sunken and submerged. The key issue in Judaism is not how much one partakes of the world, but the extent to which one makes God one's partner.

This central message is perhaps clearest in the Book of Esther. The name Esther itself comes from the Hebrew for 'hidden', and the apparent though illusory disappearance of God from His world is a pivotal theme of the book. Unique among all the books of the Hebrew Bible, God even fails to appear in the cast of characters! The events described in the Book of Esther occur in a world that is in many ways similar to the world today. Unlike the rest of the Hebrew Bible, where God is persistently performing miracles and wonders, in Esther's era He did not manifest Himself. Prophets no longer received prophecy and, as if things weren't bad enough, the Persian Empire had issued a decree to annihilate the Jews. It was at this moment that a miracle occurred that could be explained naturally. In other words, God is invisible, but He is still there, the hidden essence of every flower and gust of wind.

This belief in His omnipresence is the foundation of the Jewish institution of blessings. Before eating an apple, a religious Jew declares, 'Blessed are You Lord our God, King of the Universe, Who created the fruit of the tree.' By doing so, he brings holiness into what might otherwise be a base, animalistic activity. He forces himself to recognise God's beneficence and, simultaneously, the incredible gift that is physical presence. For this reason, Jewish festivals are replete with food, wine, and song.

Because of its rules and prescriptions, Judaism has often been accused of being weighed down by legalism. But to a Jew this weight *is* his bond with God. It guarantees that the believer need never compartmentalise himself and his religious personality. He can balance all his desires. Riches will only become his curse when they isolate him, when he owns a home into which none are invited for fear that they may sully the carpets. Asceticism will only have a place if he imagines Satan behind every dollar bill and every sexual urge.

The Purpose of Judaism is to Lose One's Faith

Unlike a faith that focuses on lofty matters, Judaism celebrates hard action. Where the Christian, for example, speaks of love, the Jew says that there can be no love without justice. Heartfelt emotions are meaningless if they do not lead to compassionate acts. The biblical narrative of Adam and Eve's sin in the Garden of Eden is central both to Judaism and Christianity. But there is an essential difference.

To the Christian, it is a story of the fall of man. Adam and Eve were given but one *mitzvah* (commandment), which they promptly transgressed. The result was that they incurred spiritual damnation. Since mankind fell as a result of this terrible sin, it could not later lift itself up to reachieve its previous spiritual elevation. Only the son of God could redeem man from his terrible fall and bring about human salvation.

For the Jew, however, the consequences of Adam's sin related more to the world that surrounded man than to man himself. The sin in Eden caused the *world*, rather than Adam and Eve, to change. For a moment, let us pause and reflect on the world inhabited by Adam and Eve from the ancient Jewish cabbalistic perspective. They lived in Eden, a world which was perfect. Where was this Eden? Was it some lofty mountaintop? Was it a heavenly abode currently hidden by a cloud? Actually, the Jewish sages explain that world inhabited by Adam and Eve is the very same world where we all dwell right this very minute. But the world which Adam and Eve knew was radically different to our own because it was perfect.

Light on Earth

In what lay the perfection of the world then? The explanation given in Jewish mystical sources is simply that the world of Adam and Eve basked in God's light. It was a world of clarity and stark moral choices. According to most biblical commentaries, well before heaven and earth were created, while the cosmos was still *tohu vavohu*, a morass of chaos and void, this light was the first thing God created. And light still is the most important thing in life. It is our symbol of hope, and there can be no question that dour national characteristics and cloudy weather are related in the same way that the natural effervescence of, say, the Italians, can be attributed to the unending sunlight.

The Garden of Eden was a perfect world because the Godly origin of the world and the guiding hand of God behind every human success was immediately reflected on the cloak of nature. Plants and animals all served as divine graffiti. Each pointed like a vector to its heavenly source. To Adam and Eve, able to discern instantly between good and evil, the world was still like a child that looks exactly like its parent. They would look at a sunset and their immediate response would be 'How wondrous are Your works, Oh Lord!' (Psalms), rather than 'Gosh, what a gorgeous scene.'

According to Judaism, it is this sensory reality that Adam and Eve removed from the world when they sinned. Plucking the fruit, they detached the world from its source. Man could now ascribe God's achievements to his own efforts, rather than to the blessing and providence of the Creator. Without fear of refutation he could openly exclaim 'My power and the might of my own hand have got me this wealth' (Deut. 8:17). As a result, man gained the capacity to deceive by masking the truth of existence.

Making the Right Choice

Taking all the good that God had given him – his love for Eve – Adam used it to act in contradiction of the divine will.

It is this volatile, chaotic mixture of good and evil that we have encountered in our world ever since: the lucidity of the primordial world has been completely lost. A man can invest his money and still never be certain that he will not lose every last penny. And it is specifically by tapping into our human competitiveness, a desire to outperform our fellow man, that we are able to generate enough income to build hospitals and orphanages. And it is specifically the scientist who yearns to win a Nobel prize who will one day find a cure for AIDS. One cannot have the blessing of children without the trials of raising them.

Pulling ever stronger, these capricious forces particularly affect our personal lives. We go into relationships hoping for the best, but also prepared, if need be, for the worst. A boy whom I met in school as a child became one of my closest friends because his parents argued as much as my own. One day at the age of fifteen, he was killed in a car accident. His parents found comfort in each other, and their marital bickering ended. That something so wondrous can result from something so ugly is too a part of the curse of Adam. Similarly, I read of a man who won the lottery, only to watch his eldest son die of a drug overdose one year later, as result of having too much cash in his pocket.

According to Judaism, therefore, in the absence of God's truth, our greatest source of pain in life is not being sure of the way forward. Husbands and wives could more easily solve the marital dilemmas they face if only they knew for certain that the person they are married to is best for them. But in the absence of such certainty, they don't try so hard to make their marriages work since they ascribe an arbitrary quality to their relationship. We search endlessly for the proper guidance to make our lives work, rarely achieving our objective satisfactorily. We often actually feel persecuted by the decisions, especially the big ones, which we have to take. Hence, after the sin of Adam and Eve, the Almighty was obliged to give the Torah at Mount Sinai, thereby giving man a code of instruction which would allow him to distinguish between the holy and the profane.

Seeing as Opposed to Believing

What religion asks of us is that we never close our eyes. This, parenthetically, is why the Nazis were the most evil men that ever stalked the planet, though there have been other mass-murderers in history. These, like Bogdan Chemielnitzky, who murdered 350,000 Jews in the years 1648-1649, at least had the decency to admit that they were blood-thirsty barbarians. They did not cover up the truth. But the Nazis claimed to carry out their programme of genocide for humanitarian reasons. They were doing humanity a favour! They were ridding the world of a pest. This is the most offensive kind of sin because it takes darkness and calls it light so that God is concealed even more.

The ultimate purpose of creation is for us to rediscover God as a tangible reality. Whereas in Christianity the acquisition of faith represents the apogee of religious attainment, in Judaism the purpose is to lose one's faith. No man, woman, or child who roams the earth should ever have to resort to faith in God. Instead, we should be able to see, with our very eyes, the materialisation of God's presence on earth and all of the Almighty's blessings. As the prophet proclaims: 'The day will come when you will see your Master.' At the giving of the Torah at Sinai, the Jews did not believe in God. They saw Him. They heard Him. They tasted Him. They smelt Him. And they experienced Him. God was as much a presence as the physical properties of the earth itself.

This transcendent light of the world will only be fully restored in the Messianic epoch when creation will be restored to its original luminescence. Until that glorious day arrives and all darkness is dispelled, Judaism attempts to restore the connection between God and his world in the most tangible possible way. The Torah and its instructions aim to take up the basic fibre of existence of this world and thereby reveal Godly reality. Even its most detailed instructions reveal the truth. The use of wool for the fulfilment of the commandment of *tzitzis* (the fringes worn by observant Jews on the corner of their clothes), for example, restores the unique divine signature which the wool once possessed in the Garden of Eden with Adam and Eve. Using cow parchment to write the Torah strengthens the link between God and the world in yet another way. By saying blessings on food observant Jews acknowledge all goodness comes from God.

Since we were not meant to believe but experience, in Jewish thought even non-belief (as opposed to covering up the truth) sustains the reality of God. A student of the great

Rabbi Zusya of Anipoli came to the Hassidic master and asked him why God allowed atheism to flourish. Worse, why did the Almighty create a world that lent credibility to atheistic claims. 'You must know, my child', answered Rabbi Zusya, 'that atheism and agnosticism are two of the most important doctrines in the world. Imagine if people were absolutely sure that God existed. They would see a hungry man in the street, but would not feed him. They would say, "Don't worry, God will provide. He will not allow the man to go hungry." But since we all sometimes question the existence of God, when we see another human being in need, we all run to help, because perhaps we are the only ones to assist him.'

1

God

Perhaps the most used and obvious term in any language is also the most mysterious. Even to speak of God risks tangling us in the nets of logical and philosophical absurdity. Who and what is God for modern day men and women who have largely forgotten Him? As Rabbi Joseph Soloveitchik wrote in a haunting passage, 'Who is He who trails me steadily, uninvited and unwanted, like an everlasting shadow, and vanishes into the recesses of transcendence the very instant I turn around to confront this numinous, awesome, and mysterious "He"?' (*The Lonely Man of Faith*). A recent statistic in *Time* magazine claimed that ninety per cent of all Americans believed in God. But on closer examination it was discovered that everyone's conception of God differed!

A Hidden God

Ancient man knew enough of his own limitations to recognise and pay homage to the lofty powers in the universe. Uncorrupted by modernity, he seems to have had a natural intuition for the transcendent and an eagerness to acknowledge his place in the order of the universe. Certainly, like us today, he lived in a world that was geared by his senses. He invented the idea of many different gods, responsible for all the great phenomena which he witnessed. There was a god of lightning, for example, and a god of oceans, or he worshipped objects such as the moon or the sun, or more tangible idols. In Greek mythology this evolved into gods who had parents and children, ate, drank, seduced and fornicated, and had uncontrollable desires and passions. And latterly, in the age of Newton and Descartes, man's ancient homage developed into deism, the doctrine that God, having created the world, withdrew himself from it completely, leaving it to run by its own internal devices.

However, because Judaism sensed another truth – a truth similar to the one modern science discovered by teasing a finely grained understanding from the inanimate world around us – paganism and idolatry were repugnant to it from the start. It passionately proclaimed God's utter mystery. From the beginning, it maintained He can not only be found at the summit of mountains, but can also be grasped as much in the soft colours of the rainbow, the cool shade of a tree or the mighty eruption of a volcano. Or, in terms of the scripture, when God appeared to Elijah, the prophet, first 'there was a great wind, so strong that it was splitting mountains and breaking rocks in pieces before the Lord, but the Lord was not in the earthquake; and after the earthquake a fire, but the Lord was not in the fire; and after the fire a still small voice.' God could be found everywhere man looked.

The most important Jewish belief about God is rooted in the idea that the most hidden forces in the universe are simultaneously the most powerful. It is for this reason that the Jewish order of the Hebrew Bible is different from the Christian order. In the Jewish order, the five books of Moses are followed by the prophets, and only then by scripture and apocrypha, following a consistent theme. God begins with a strong revelation in the books of Moses; no longer shows Himself but at least speaks to the prophets; and then ends up

only as a source of inspiration for the later books of Psalms, Esther, Proverbs, and Song of Songs. It was necessary to show the Jews that God was not only at Sinai. Nor was He only engaged in conversation with the wise and the pious. Rather, 'there is no place devoid of His presence.'

In the perception of this truth also lies the greatness of Abraham, the most senior Jewish patriarch. As the first in Judaism, the young Abraham put forward the idea that all existence emanated from a source whose energy and presence underlay all of creation. According to the Talmud, he did so by a process of logical elimination. At first, witnessing the brightness and brilliance of the sun, and how its warmth is vital to all forms of life, Abraham prostrated himself before its rays and worshipped it as the supreme deity. But in the evening, he changed his mind. The moon, launching a rebellion, assisted by the heavenly host of the stars, defeated the sun, causing its brilliance to cease to shine. Abraham then worshipped the moon as the conqueror of the sun. Clearly the moon was a far more powerful deity. But when in the morning the sun rallied its forces and defeated the moon, Abraham began to worship the air around him. Surrounding living beings from all sides, the air encompassed all of creation and surely was the great deity which he so hoped to discover. But he then pondered man's superiority to the air. While being porous and having many bodily cavities, man was able to contain air and breath, thus proving he was its master. However, having seen the lowliness of man, and the repeated errors which he could commit, Abraham was not about to worship himself or any other man. It was then that the great truth finally dawned upon him. He began to understand how all of nature was a veil which masked the presence of the deity, and how man must learn to apprehend the hidden Creator.

The Meaning of a Hidden God

Three thousand years later, modern science acknowledges the very same paradox of the most hidden being the most powerful. Physics has shown us in the past centuries what ancient men never knew: that our universe is an intricate organisation which follows a systematic, at any rate mathematical, regularity whose deepest structure and force can only be postulated and not directly perceived. Coming from a different perspective, psychoanalysis has demonstrated that the forces that shape our personalities are subliminal impulses, defences, memories, and sometimes fears that reside deep within the psyche. These forces have greater influence over us than we often care to acknowledge. Both these disciplines have taught us to rely on the authority of other findings, rather than the immediate evidence presented to us by our senses and everyday life experience.

The modern world seems unable to draw any practical lessons from this knowledge that science has amassed. Just look around you. Favouring short-termism, we fail to take account of the meaning of our deeper desires. Today we see a world that is obsessed with the immediate gratification of the senses. We no longer have the spiritual conviction that ancient man had, and we are no longer aware of our own place in the universe. Parents, for example, no longer primarily desire their children to be ethical and decent. 'As long as my daughter is happy' has become the common refrain of modern education. And men and women define success by their professional achievements rather than by the quality of their relationships.

But the invisibility of God has always had radical, immediate, implications for every aspect of life in Jewish thought.

Once, I tried to patch together a marriage and told the husband that he must be more tender to his wife. 'But what should I do,' he told me, 'when the things she is doing are just wrong? Should I not try to correct her, and ignore her faults, just for the sake of my marriage? Wrong is wrong!' The error he made is that, like most of us, he only looked for mistakes, discarding his more fundamental desire to have a loving companion, however imperfect. Like all powerful spiritual desires that determine our lives, love and peace are subtle qualities that are easily swamped by the harshness and raw emotion of argument unless we make an effort to connect the one with the other.

Predicated on the pivotal concept that man was created to serve the one true God, Judaism has a two-fold purpose. First, to make God known. Second, to teach man how He wishes to be served. Like Abraham, man must realise that God is everywhere, that He is all around him and is the source of all life and existence. A man or wife who comes home and finds a hot meal waiting would be a fool, not to mention a highly unromantic partner, if all he or she can see is a plate of food rather than the affection with which it was produced. Through our understanding of God, we'll grow accustomed to seeing that even in the everyday instances of our life, the key to our existence lies in seeing the subtle within the obvious.

How God is Known

In many ways we are at a point in time similar to the Jews in Sinai. The enormity of the problem lies in the fact that our vision has become blunted.

Imagine speaking to a young man of twenty years, who is

all hormonal and dating a beautiful young woman. What is important to him is his desire for sex rather than love. Speak to him about how much more special love is than sex, and he will think that you have taken leave of your senses. He is not yet old enough, not sufficiently experienced, to appreciate the sublimity of love. Indeed, if someone were to suggest that he refrain from sex with the woman in question in order to wait for love, he would think the person even more crazy. Sex provides immediate gratification.

God's demand from the Jewish people in uttering the first of Ten Commandments, 'I am the Lord your God who has taken you out from Egypt', was an extraordinary order. Here the Almighty was asking the Jews to put the subtle and the abstract before the material and the concrete. But the Jewish people forsook the worship of the sun and the moon – both of which provide instant sensory comfort and benefits – allowing them to develop an appreciation and love for subtlety and gentleness which took the other nations of the world far longer to acquire.

Unity

Since we are created in the 'image of God', it is interesting to note that our understanding of Him reflects what we think about ourselves. There can be no definitive description of God, according to Judaism. The Talmud relates the following story: a Caesar said to Rabbi Joshua ben Hananiah: 'I want to see your God, Rabbi Joshua.' 'You cannot see Him, Caesar.' 'Nevertheless, I want to see Him.' So Rabbi Joshua had Caesar stand facing the sun during the summer solstice and said to Him, 'Look directly into the sun, Caesar.' 'I cannot.' Rabbi Joshua then said, 'If you say of the sun, which is only one of the servants standing before the Holy One Blessed be He, I cannot look directly at it, how much less can you look at the brilliance of the Divine Presence.' (Hullin 60a)

If we want to know God, we cannot say what He is, only what He isn't. But while we cannot give a blind man a positive description about colour, we can tell him that it is not something he can feel or taste. The same is true of the deity. We can say that God is infinite, or not finite. He has no limitations. By stripping away many of the adjectives which we use to describe empirical phenomena, we can come to know something of His essence. Many of the great Jewish sages even maintained that we could not say that God is compassionate, wise, forgiving, and the like, since this too involves positive description and is an arrogant claim on the part of mortal man to know the unknowable. Rather, all we can say is that God is not unkind, not unwise, and not unforgiving.

Within this context, the most essential Jewish concept about God is His absolute and indivisible unity. As Maimonides writes, 'God is one … The oneness of any of the single things existent in the universe is unlike His Unit. He is not one as a species since this includes numerous individuals; nor one as a body since this is divisible into parts and sections, but a Unity which is unique in the world.' Thus, importantly, the universe has no competing powers which oppose God's sovereignty according to Judaic theology, nor has God created the universe and abandoned its running to the laws of nature. Judaism's war against dualism has been as thorough as its war against atheism.

The notion of demonic forces that wage war against the deity or deities is wholly alien to Judaic theology. Even Satan is no more than the heavenly prosecutor, serving the divine purpose. The classical Jewish mystical text, the Zohar, sees Satan as a divine agent, whose mission is to exercise every charm in the seduction of man, thereby providing him with choice. In understanding the role of Satan, the Zohar gives the analogy of a prostitute who is sent by the king to test the moral stature of his son, the crown prince. Even while employing all her charm in an effort to seduce the prince, she inwardly hopes that he will not succumb.

Immanence and Transcendence

With good reason, Judaism rejects the two main currents in world philosophy in understanding God. One underscores God's otherness or transcendence, how He has nothing in common with the world and serves merely as its ultimate detached Source. The other underscores God's immanence, or accessibility. Represented most categorically in Western philosophy by Spinoza, the latter maintains that God is identical with the world and nature – the pantheistic view that nature is sacred and holy. (It was for this utterly heretical view that Spinoza was the subject of the last great excommunication within the Jewish faith, carried out by the Jewish court of Amsterdam in the year 1656.)

The transcendent school of thought, represented most typically by Descartes and Newton, will accept only that the world is the creation of a God so powerful and aloof that by necessity He is removed from it, having set the mechanism of creation in motion. This view of God is the one most common among today's watered-down believers. They affirm that God is indeed the Creator, but regulating world events would be beneath His infinite glory and dignity. When most people speak of mother nature, this is exactly what they mean, a God who is cloaked and veiled by instinct, quiet and indifferent to human activity, completely unresponsive to the pain of human tragedy.

Upon closer inspection, both conceptions of God – as either wholly transcendent or wholly immanent – emerge as deficient in important ways. The transcendant God of creation seems inherently unimpressive. Why pray to God at all if He is nothing more than a distant big brother? If He is a stoical God who is calm and silent in the face of human misery and famine how can He endear Himself to vulnerable humans who look to God for comfort and salvation? The other, immanent, conception is similarly flawed. If God is synonymous with nature, as in Spinozan pantheism, that means that we humans are alone in an impersonal universe, abandoned to the elements. Without a transcendent God, who can hear our cry? Religion, in the sense of establishing a relationship with the deity, becomes an absurdity, for a God who is only historical is also too unpredictable and volatile to be of any use to humanity.

Bearing in mind these considerations, Judaism offers the world a knowledge of God that is *both* transcendent *and* immanent. Based on the ancient cabbalistic principle of *tzim-tzum* (or contraction), Judaism explains that God is both the Creator and the Regulator of history, encompassing the world from without but also animating it from within. He is the Creator, an impersonal God who fills and regulates the infinite expanse of space. But equally, He is a personal God, attentive to human needs and mindful of human cries. Thus, both King and Comforter, Master and Redeemer, Father and Friend, Disciplinarian and Lover, He reaches out to man in his travail, comforting the bereaved, healing the sick, and establishing a covenant of mutual love with man in which the earth is never forsaken. He can indeed alter suffering, but even when He appears silent He is quietly present in the cataclysm, comforting those who ache.

God and His World

But why indeed should we believe in a God who is both Creator of life and Regulator of human affairs, source of all being and guiding force behind history, particularly today? There is little unity around us. The byword of the age is that men are from Mars and women are from Venus. Like continental drift, with each temperamental eruption people seem to float further and further apart. The rate of divorce in the Western world is careering out of control, and young people find no compelling reason to marry. We are witnessing the breakdown of race relations. Eighty per cent of black students today at American Universities choose to dorm with other black students, and this black–white divide in the United States continues to widen. Rife with divisive nationalist sentiment, in the Middle East there seems to be no real peace ahead for the Jews and Arabs. In the former Yugoslavia, the ethnic factions continue to wage war against each other.

I think the answer to all this lies in our fundamental belief in equality (predicated in turn on the belief that we all emanate from one source). As a Rabbi living in the modern age of space exploration, I have often been asked whether or not Judaism believes in the existence of extraterrestrial life. Maybe. But, even if we could conceivably contact other worlds, the question remains: what would we have in common with them? If organisms on Jupiter have evolved from separate cosmic dust to the slime-cell origin of mankind on

earth, then, curiosity aside, what difference does it make whether or not these creatures exist? They are not our brothers, aside from a cognitive capacity to evaluate each other.

In her film, *Contact*, actress Jody Foster travels to a galaxy billions of light years away and encounters a civilisation which tells her that they have been around for aeons. The only thing which makes the darkness and emptiness of space bearable, they contend, is the fact that there are other creatures with whom they can share contact. But then why can they not find that same affinity even with stones and rocks? Only if there is a God, and we are all united through having this common ancestry, does the search for extraterrestrial life become a meaningful search on the part of kin to assuage a loneliness resulting from being deposited in an endless and mostly empty universe. The search becomes like that for a long-lost relative, or an adopted child's search for his biological parents.

This, ultimately, is the only source for the belief in the equality of all mankind. After all, where does this strange belief, which we so take for granted, ultimately stem from? Few would claim to be the intellectual equals of Albert Einstein, or the athletic equals of Carl Lewis. Virginia Kelly, who died in 1994, had two sons. The elder is President Bill Clinton of the United States. The younger is Roger Clinton, who has had a history of drug addiction, business failures, and is accused of being a deadbeat dad. If she were to be asked who is more important to her, is there anyone who would believe that she would say that by virtue of his vast achievement, her elder son is more loved? The very idea is preposterous for every mother loves her children equally. In truth, people are all equal by virtue of the fact that we are all

God's children and that in His eyes, we are all the same. This may be an unfashionable thought, but it is elegant and simple.

'My Ways Are Not Your Ways'

Approaching the conception of God and man from a philosophical point of view, the ancient Jewish mystics said that with creation the Almighty contracted His infinite presence in what is known as *tzim-tzum*, condensation. This contraction yields a *makum panui*, or empty space. This space is not empty in a literal sense, since God is omnipresent. Rather, it is like a condensation in which God's essence is present but concealed, affording man the illusion of freedom. The world is brought into existence within this 'empty space' thereby hiding the immediacy of God's presence and allowing man the real opportunity for freedom of choice.

What this belief means in practical terms is that Judaism has a deeply rooted holistic philosophy of existence and life. Ultimately nothing is contradictory. Everything can be reduced to one essential point, connecting all organic and inorganic matter, every idea, every phenomenon, and every human being. Man and the world around him can integrate all diverse and often conflicting inner impulses and orchestrate them into one effective system, because neither the world nor the soul of man is diffuse.

At first glance, this may seem interesting but unremarkable. But if we take a further look we can see that this belief galvanises philosophical debate. As Isaiah Berlin writes: 'There exists a great chasm between those, on one side, who relate everything to a single central vision, one system, less or more coherent and articulate, in terms of which they understand, think and feel – a single, universal, organising principle in terms of which all that they are and say has significance – and, on the other side, those who pursue many ends, often unrelated and even contradictory, connected, if at all, only in some de facto way, for some psychological or physiological cause, related to no moral or aesthetic principle.'

Most – if not all – Western thinkers belong to the 'non-unitarian' side that Berlin identifies. Philosophers such as Locke, Hobbes and Rousseau pioneered the concept of 'original position' to explain and to justify particular social structures. Some of them conceive man as being fundamentally noble and free, others take him to be, in essence, brutal and animalistic. But, essentially, what these 'original' positions show is that the human condition is broken up into (at least) two parts, with man torn between them. He is never a free agent.

The fissiparous nature of Western philosophy is clearest in Hegel. According to him, human beings, like animals, have natural needs and a desire for objects outside themselves, such as food, drink, shelter, and above all the preservation of their own lives and bodies. Man differs fundamentally from the animals, because in addition he desires the desire of other men, that is, he wants to be 'recognised'. This worth, in the first instance, is related to a primordial willingness to risk his life in a struggle with his fellow man. By staking their lives in a fight to the death, primordial combatants seek to make the other 'recognise' their humanness. But as they battle, the natural fear of death begins to inhibit both combatants, and the one who submits to this fear and surrenders becomes a slave to the other more heroic combatant. Thus, though man is able to overcome his most basic animal instincts – the instinct for self-preservation being the most important – for the sake of more lofty, abstract principles and goals, at the heart of the matter lie aggression and animal needs.

Judaism too has an 'original position', which is the story of Adam's creation. But at its most fundamental level, the story of human existence is not about power, nor about prestige. It is about a human being, endowed with free will, responding to the word of God. The rabbis point out that both the lower animals and the higher angels have the same Hebrew name, *chayot*. Stretched within this continuum of existence is man, halfway between angel and beast. By exercising his freedom of choice, man can either rise to the level of the angels, or descend to the level of the beast. In His love for man God has, so to speak, condensed an area of freedom in which man can elect to do right or wrong (Deut. 5:26; 30:17). His freedom is absolute. In rabbinic language: 'Everything is in the power of Heaven except the reverence of Heaven' (Ber. 33b).

In the famous biblical tragedy of Job, God reproaches Job's friends, who were on His side; but Job is rewarded despite his searing indictment of God's actions. The God-man relationship flowers in an evolutionary process of education. Man is gradually weaned from his own inhumanity, from atrocities, like human sacrifice (Gen. 22:2-14), from bestial conduct, and from wronging his fellow man. The eternal fires of hell are never used as a deterrent – though punishment of the wicked after death is obscurely mentioned (Isa. 66:24; Dan. 12:2) – nor is paradise used as an inducement. Man must choose God for love of God and because He is the truth, and for no ulterior motive. Every other inducement is a subtle form of idolatry and self-serving goals.

How God is Served

If, having been created in 'the image of God', man, like his Creator, is entirely free, how is God's unity of creation still relevant to man's freedom? The answer is that the unity of God finds its corollary in a radical social philosophy of peace and integration. The ultimate fraternity of man, amidst endless internecine warfare, is not just a possibility, but an inevitability, since all stem from, and are encompassed by, the deity. Jews and Arabs may yet conduct war for centuries to come, but ultimately they will lay down their swords and beat them into ploughshares, because an underlying harmony permeates their individual identities. Man is capable of restoring that pristine spirituality by hating sin and practising acts of loving kindness. Man is even capable of orchestrating the conflict between his mind and heart. Within man's freedom to act, the concept of unity is present as his guiding principle.

So far we have examined the Jewish *definition* of God. Fundamentally, however, God is met in a direct existential encounter, which is true revelation. The medieval scholar Judah Halevi argued in the *Kuzari*, that God is apprehended existentially far more than he is comprehended rationally. What he meant to say with this is that God is always found through the great historical events of revelation, rather than merely in the minds of the philosophers.

Like every religion, Judaism has always utilised and appealed to rational deductive proofs for the existence of God in an attempt to establish an intellectual concept of faith and religious certitude. Indeed, a certain proximity to Him can be established with philosophical insight and knowledge. But intellectual speculation within Judaism is never a panacea or replacement for the religious relationship itself which is communion with God, and is higher than knowledge. Indeed, it was Maimonides, the great Jewish thinker and arch-rationalist, who compared man's obligation to love God with the intense, all-consuming love that a love-sick man feels for a woman. And the ancient rabbis saw the highly erotic book of 'Songs of Songs' as an all-encompassing metaphor for the way man must feel for the Creator.

Even we who count ourselves among the devout have lost track of the meaning of this. Sure, we may pay Him token homage in keeping with the flimsy practice of our receding religious faith. But why don't we recognise that it is in God's power to make our lives successful? Why don't we today pray to God as if the offering of that prayer will make or break our careers? How many of us who are religious today relate to God, not just as some spiritual abstraction, but rather as Parent, Master, and tender Friend accompanying us through all of life's vicissitudes? The prophet Micah expressed it succinctly: 'He has told you, O mortal, what is good; and what does the Lord require of you but to do justice, and to love kindness, and to walk humbly with your God?' (6:8).

No wonder that in this frosty atmosphere where God remains such a stranger religion has died such a horrible death. The great and tortured novelist Franz Kafka penned his father a letter, which the latter never read due to his sudden death. It said, 'It would have been thinkable that we might both have found each other in Judaism or that we might have begun from there in harmony. But what sort of Judaism was it that I got from you? ... It was impossible to make a child, over-acutely observant from sheer nervousness, understand that the few flimsy gestures you performed in the name of Judaism, and with an indifference in keeping with their flimsiness, could have any higher meaning. For you they had meaning as little souvenirs of earlier times, and that is why you wanted to pass them on to me. But since they no longer had any intrinsic value, even for you, you could do this only through persuasion or threat.' These lines could be written by almost any child growing up in a Jewish or Christian home for whom religion has become a burden, a dead carcass to bear, rather than a fountain of living waters.

A Spiritual *and* Temporal God

The world's religions have various ways of portraying the faith experience. In Judaism, it is conceived as being in a relationship with God, both on a national and personal level. The 613 commandments of the Torah are the strands that hold together the relationship the man of faith has with God. Judaism is not about simply submitting before God, but rather about man joining God as a partner in the unfolding drama of creation, giving succour to the needy, love to the forlorn, and food to the hungry of the nation. Biblical references abound of God as the bridegroom of the nation of Israel, and the Jews as his chosen bride. This imagery reaches its dramatic and powerful apex in the incomparable love poem, 'Song of Songs', written by King Solomon, which the ancient rabbis interpreted as allegorical of the love between God and the Jewish people.

The cabbalists even used sexual imagery to describe the union of the Creator with the Jews. Indeed, many of the Jewish rituals at a wedding ceremony are derived from the giving of the Law at Mount Sinai. The wedding canopy itself results from the Talmudic legend that God draped the mountain over the nation of Israel as a sign of His protection. Similarly, the bridegroom waits under the canopy for the arrival of his bride, just as the thunder and lightning, representing God's presence, preceded the Jews at Mount Sinai. In the same way that Moses ascended the mountain to bring God's 'bride' to Him, so too a Jewish bride today is led to the canopy by an escort, usually consisting of her parents. Man requires a relationship with God in all aspects of his life, and religion seeks to maintain as close a relationship as possible. In the beautiful words of the great medieval Jewish poet, Rabbi Judah Halevi, 'When far from Thee, I die, while yet in life; but if I cling to Thee, I live, though I should die' (*Kuzari*).

In the Cabbalah, the idea of the God-man relationship mirroring that of husband and wife finds its most strident expression. According to the cabbalists, God, as mysterious as this may seem, has needs, much as man has needs. For any marriage to be successful, it is necessary for husband and wife not only to celebrate birthdays and anniversaries, but also to greet each other every day. Likewise, man must proffer gratitude to his Creator every waking day and aspire to know God in all his ways. And God informs the Jewish people that He requires them to accommodate His will.

The basis of every relationship between two parties is the willingness to accommodate one another's needs. The very act of entering into a relationship is an undeclared yet tacit acceptance of the simple fact that no desire of one's beloved is trivial or irrelevant. Thus, the Jewish man of faith who dismisses observance of the dietary restrictions because they do not lend themselves to his rational apprehension, is no different to a husband who refuses to buy his wife flowers because he cannot understand why she should crave something that will be dead tomorrow. Even the offer to buy her a ruby or emerald still amounts to a rejection of her intrinsic will and, therefore, worth. Such a man is incapable of being in a relationship because he expects everyone to be his clone.

Real love in Jewish thought goes beyond attempting to understand each other; it involves an inner experience which translates externally in a desire to cater to the wishes of one's beloved. Hence, the first Jewish step in knowing God is an unconditional acceptance of His expressed will, although it may not make sense. This idea may seem foreign to today's men and women who prize communication within a relationship above all else. But those whose marriages last understand there can be nothing more romantic, and no better way to make someone feel cherished, than to respect, anticipate and respond to their (seemingly irrational) needs and desires.

God is an End and Never a Means

Judaism is a religion which is profoundly deiocentric. Every human action should be impelled by a love and fear of God, and should be undertaken for the express purpose of fulfilling His will. This means that in any discussion concerning the deity, God must always be perceived as the end, and never the means. He is neither an instrument to human self-fulfilment, nor a road by which man may achieve nirvana, salvation, everlasting life, or any other ultimate reward.

In Christianity, Jesus is portrayed principally as the road to salvation: a belief in Jesus redeems man from the inferno of hell. However, in Judaism, God is described as the ultimate perfection and the ultimate end. Man cannot use God to fulfil his own ends, however noble or worthy, and he must embrace His service with no ulterior motives. God is not an escape route from oblivion. No woman would be impressed with a man who proposes marriage declaring that he believes that the experience of marriage will mature him and give him direction in life. A woman wants to know that a man wants to marry her for one reason alone: because he loves her, because she is special. Man must approach God with the same level of selflessness and desire.

Professor Y. Liebowitz has pointed out that this difference between Judaism and Christianity is best summed up in their quintessential symbols of sacrifice and faith. The archetypal service of God in Judaism is captured in the Akeida, the binding of Isaac, in which Abraham was called upon by God to sacrifice everything, even his own son, to God. The Creator is depicted as the highest end to which all things must be dedicated. Contrast this with the highest religious symbol of Christianity which is undoubtedly the Crucifixion. Here, it is *God* who is prepared to sacrifice His only son so that man can be cleansed of sin. The blood of the divine son dripping from the cross is a sacrifice on the part of the deity for the sake of His human children.

There is no guarantee that loving and serving God will lead to any higher reward or even ennoblement of character. Judaism has not used portraits of demonic suffering in hell, or even luscious pleasures in heaven, to attract adherents or inspire its faithful. Most of the discussion in the Talmud about where the soul goes after death is surrounded by misty and contradictory speculation on the part of the rabbis. The rabbis never wanted anyone to serve God on the basis that they would one day be rewarded, so their discussion of the afterlife is extremely limited. There are no beautiful virgins who will pleasure the Jewish believer as there are in the Muslim heaven, and one may safely assume that one's mother will still be heard complaining about not being cared for enough. The ancient rabbis taught: 'Do not be like servants who serve their master for the sake of receiving a reward, but rather be like servants who serve their master without the intent of receiving a reward; and let the fear of heaven be upon you.' One should serve God out of love of truth. If modern man starts here, like the Jews in Sinai, he will have made his first step towards the light.

2

The Sabbath

Any traveller through Christian Europe will see the great monuments that the believers of old built for their Lord. Wondrous cathedrals of unmatched splendour rise toward the heavens. Many places of worship, in fact, from Islamic mosques to Buddhist shrines, offer exotic displays of lustrous gold, sumptuous, intricately carved precious stones, and translucent spaces pierced by rays of sunlight and crowned by soaring spires. Even today, new awe-inspiring structures with the most dazzling state of the art technology and rare materials are being financed by the devout and consecrated by their clergy.

In contrast, Judaism has never had such magnificent cathedrals. Certainly, there are some beautiful synagogues in existence and there was, of course, the great Temple in Jerusalem that was destroyed first by the Babylonians, and then by the Romans. Indeed, the very land of Israel, a space consecrated by God as a holy land, is central to the Jewish religion. But, since the Jews have not been on their land for most of Jewish history, they have not had a Temple.

Rather, Jewish religion has thrived on cathedrals in time rather than cathedrals of space. Dividing the empirical world into three fundamental components – time, space, and mankind – the purpose of the Jewish faith has always been the consecration of all three through man using time in the service of the Creator in His appointed places. Rather than focus his mind on a specific location, the man of faith is meant to cordon off times in which God is experienced as a tangible and living reality. The very first time the word holy is used in the Bible is in connection with the Sabbath day: 'So God blessed the seventh day and made it holy, because on it God rested from all the work that He had done in creation' (Gen. 2:3). Similarly, the first commandment given to the Jewish people before their emergence from the crucible of Egypt was the sanctification of the new moon and new lunar month. They were to witness the monthly rebirth of the moon and consecrate the time as Rosh Chodesh, the first day of the new Jewish month.

When Judaism does pay attention to a geographical location the concept is used very differently. In other religions, generally, the location is first chosen for a place of worship, and only then do actions undertaken within, such as prayer or acts of confession, become sacred. In other words, through the sanctuary time is consecrated.

But in Judaism the reverse is true. It is time that sanctifies space. Judaism is obsessed with holy and special moments, in the same way that the bridge or field where a couple enjoyed their first kiss will always be special to them. It is the supernatural events which have come to pass in a certain place that lend that location its solemnity. Mount Moriah, the domain where the Temple was built in Jerusalem, was sacred because, according to tradition, it was there that God took clay from the earth, fashioned it into the guise of a man, breathed life into it, and called that being Adam. On the same site, many centuries later, Abraham was commanded to bring his son Isaac as a sacrifice to God. The site (space) became holy because of the great event (time) that happened there.

Taking this one step further, in Judaism the most exquisite

beauty is found in the towering imagination that supports the Sabbath and the Jewish festivals. These cathedrals in time are the equivalents of the opulent exuberance of shrines found in other religions. Because man, according to the Bible, is conditioned to embrace time, he must make space for its enjoyment rather than time for the creation of religious spaces. Instead of erecting altars, the Jew works in order to save up money and celebrate sacred and precious moments with family, friends, and community. Instead of spending 'time' in the acquisition of 'space', Judaism argues that we must do the opposite. A loving parent will spend the large sum necessary to fly his daughter back from University so that they can celebrate festive moments together. Space, or property, must be used to acquire time.

This is what Jewish life is about: seizing the moment and living for glorious times as opposed to conquering vast tracts of land and seizing glorious works of art. The Jewish year is like a spiral in which man continually comes back to the same periods of sanctity each of which evokes a different season of the spirit and calls forth memories of an earlier period in his development and that of the Jewish nation. 'Remember the days of old, consider the years long past' (Deut. 32:7). Thus, the Sabbath is a day of relationships, prayer, and enlightenment. A similar idea pervades the festivals and each represents time set aside for reflection on the profound architecture of life.

There are obvious advantages in building and beautifying shrines of the imagination. To go to a holy place, one must undertake a long and arduous journey, a pilgrimage in which one leaves behind one's family and one's home in order to enter the holy place. But to enter into a holy time, man need do nothing save remain passive, idle in his natural surroundings, until the sacred moment overtakes him. When it seizes him, like a boat rising in the high tide man is uplifted and transported by the magic of the spiritual moment in the company of those dearest to him. In his daily life the man of faith can at all times dedicate himself to an understanding of the preciousness of the moment. He may act immediately when it is needed most, rather than having to wait and look back in prayer.

Life is filled with too many precious moments. The time we parents have with our children when they are young and adorable is fleeting. If not captured now, it will soon be lost forever. Nor can we work ourselves to the point of distraction, where all our time is dominated by the pursuit of success. Money should be used to buy us time, to acquire sacred moments with parents, siblings, spouse, children, and friends. A wealthy man once said to me that the only real blessing of wealth is the freedom it buys its holder. One undermines that blessing and turns it into a curse when one allows one's lifestyle to become a gilded cage, when we become enslaved to the glitter of our fortunes and the power of our jobs.

Today's Sabbath

The seven-day cycle by which all humanity today reckons time and regulates its affairs undoubtedly has its origin in the Hebrew Bible. A day of rest, devoted to spiritual renewal and family, was utterly unknown in the ancient world. In fact, the Jews suffered ridicule on account of their day of rest from some of Rome's most prolific literary figures, including Seneca, Juvenal, and Tacitus. Nonetheless, attempts to change the Jewish pattern and move the day of rest into a different time-frame have all met with failure. As recently as the French Revolution, when all things were changed to a decimal system, the fathers of the revolution tried to reconstruct the week into ten instead of seven days, with no success. It seems a fact of life that for all of us, throughout the world, the holy Sabbath has become the goal of the week.

But does this also mean that we, Jews and non-Jews alike, have really understood its purpose? People generally believe the Sabbath was instituted to renew one's energies so that one might avoid exhaustion in the coming six days. Even Leon Trotsky said that he would preserve the Sabbath in the atheistic culture of the Soviet Union, because all workers needed to rest. Our modern business-oriented and money-making world couldn't agree more. Rest and relaxation are seen as servicing the needs of the economy as workers will be more productive if they are given time to refresh and renew their energy.

Can we really say that this conception of the Sabbath as a time to recuperate from our daily toil has worked? Certainly, modern man is very productive, no doubt more productive than ever. In the modern age of the entrepreneur, the gates of wealth and success have been opened to nearly everyone, and there are millions of runners hell-bent on reaching the finishing line. But have we managed to balance these opportunities? I have grown accustomed to having to wait three or four months to meet up with friends just for a simple dinner, such is the congestion of both our diaries. Most people suffer from sleep deprivation as they fight to cram more and more into their hectic schedules. The ring of mobile phones drills a hole through our ears, while e-mails that must be answered clock up, and faxes and post stream through our in-trays. And just when we thought we could relax, we must travel hundreds of miles for an urgent business meeting.

As rabbi at Oxford I have seen how today's young students suffer from this work-induced malady. When I ask the students what they intend to be upon graduating from Oxford, they usually tell me that they will be either investment bankers, lawyers, or doctors. I then point out to them that they have told me what they are planning to *do* – engage in international finance, practise law, practise medicine – but not *what* or *whom* they intend to be. Will their title 'solicitor' come before 'father', 'son', 'friend' or 'Jew'?

The greatest consequence of our productive but harried lifestyle is that the urgent is always placed before the important. This is not because we don't see it happening. Modern-day man is no fool. We know what is important. It is just that we simply never have any time for it. I once overheard a conversation between a young mother in her thirties and her elderly mother. The woman complained that it is so hard to raise children these days. Her mother responded ironically, 'In my day it was much harder. We had no television.' Studies show that American parents give their children on average just three uninterrupted minutes of attention per day. This is a shocking figure, but it is easy to picture how it happens. You sit down to play with your children or to read them a story. Suddenly, you notice that it is now seven o'clock, and there is a very important item on the evening news which you just cannot miss. Later, when you return to resume your time with your children, you look at your watch and remember that the gym will only be open for another half hour.

'My Son is the Sabbath'

The Jewish Sabbath is far removed from this stale under-standing of rest that would have us believe that moments for ourselves merely serve a higher goal and should take a back seat to whatever else we are doing. In Judaism, it is the six days of work that are all a preparation for the one glorious, truly holy day of the week. As the celebrated medieval Jewish pietist and sage, Rabbi Judah He-Hasid, said: 'One who goes to sleep on the Sabbath should not say, "Let us sleep so that we can do our work when the Sabbath is over", but rather let him say, "Let us rest for today is the Sabbath"' (*Sefer Hasidim*).

For eleven years my wife and I have provided Sabbath meals and hospitality for Oxford students, hosting up to one hundred students at the L'Chaim Centre on a weekly basis. What is particularly interesting is that scores of non-Jewish students come to share the Sabbath meal with us. Over eleven years this must add up to hundreds, maybe thousands, of Gentiles who have now shared our Sabbath. By their own admission, they have never experienced anything like it, and for many the Sabbath meal became the only moment during the week when they felt totally at ease and set free from the pressure exerted on them at Oxford.

The real beauty of the Sabbath is that for its duration there simply is nothing urgent. Instead of winding down to a lower gear, we should be elevated to a higher plane of reality. The ancient rabbis speak of the seven days of creation. But we all know that creation took place in six, not seven days. On the seventh day God did not create but remained totally passive. The Talmud explains that at the completion of six days the world was still missing one pivotal ingredient: 'When the

Sabbath came, peace came with it.' Following in His footsteps, on that day we should be appreciating and indulging in the passive side of our natures.

The Sabbath has its own serenity which is difficult to describe and must be experienced. A family sits down at the Sabbath table to partake of the Sabbath feast. The father makes the blessing of a cup of wine, which is then drunk by the entire family. They wash their hands for the eating of the challah, the special braided Sabbath bread, and they then indulge in the sheer peace and pleasure of a meal together. Suddenly, the phone rings. But this time, nobody rushes to pick it up. It is forbidden. It is nine o'clock and time for the evening news. But nobody runs to turn on the television. The world can wait. The family is impervious to events outside the home, for the only reality is the warmth, love, and kinship which they share around the table with each other and their guests. A cocoon of holiness has been created which cannot be invaded by ephemeral concerns. Conversation does not concern the latest film and football scores. Rather, the children read aloud what they have learned at school of the weekly Bible portion, and the family speaks of God as a close and reliable friend.

Passiveness on God's Day

There is no doubt that one of the most recurring themes of the Bible is the prohibition against the performance of work on the Sabbath. But what kind of work is prohibited on the Sabbath if it is not just rest from work? Even religious-minded people today reject the classical interpretation of work. They feel that in chasing leisurely pursuits, they are not desecrating the law or spirit of the Sabbath. In a public debate with a leading reform rabbi, my opponent said that it was ludicrous that in the modern age we should continue to ban things like lighting fires or driving on the Sabbath, i.e. activities which do not involve exertion. He argued that the Sabbath day was a day of rest, and therefore, anything which a person found restful, such as gardening or going to a music concert, would be considered in the spirit of the Sabbath day.

In reality, the Sabbath is a day in which man rests from his own physical creativity. As I said above, God created heaven and the earth in six days. On the seventh day He rested, and commanded man henceforth to do the same. What this means is that on the Sabbath we rest from the kind of work which God undertook in the original six days, namely creative labour. Our ability today to control disease and prevent floods bears witness to the considerable progress we have made in our race to become masters of nature. But in this effort to subdue nature and express our mastery over the elements, one great risk looms over us continually, namely, the possibility, and even probability, that we forget that we too are *creatures*, as well as *creators*.

Endowed by God with an enormous capacity for creativity, man can easily begin to deify himself. Not too long ago, art focused on religious subjects. I do not believe that the choice of this subject matter over any other can be intrinsically better. But consider this fact. It does demonstrate that mankind once felt the obligation to devote his creative energy to praising the Creator and His handiwork. Now it seems that art as a unique creation has become idolised. I remember that when the Uffizi gallery was car-bombed by terrorists in 1993, the newspapers first gave a detailed report on which masterpieces had been damaged. Only later did they mention that people had died in the blast as well. Such misplaced treasuring of human craftsmanship is precisely what the Sabbath is designed to combat. Art should ennoble and enhance human life, never supplant it.

It is for this reason that, according to Judaism, we must rest on the Sabbath from any kind of creative labour. For orthodox Jews, there are many thousands of tributary forms of work which are prohibited under the thirty-nine archetypal categories of work. Some of the more common prohibitions on the Sabbath include: ploughing, sowing, reaping, baking, bleaching, dyeing, spinning, weaving, tying a knot, tearing, trapping or hunting, building, demolishing, kindling a fire, writing, erasing, sewing, grinding, cooking, sifting, and putting the finishing touch to a newly manufactured article. In addition, carrying from a private to a public domain is prohibited and the observant Jew therefore does not walk into the street on the Sabbath with anything in his pockets.

Why, you may ask? Unlike the other forbidden actions, this does not involve man's mastery over creation, since there is no material change in the object concerned. However, in the same way that the ceasing from any kind of creative labour acknowledges God as the source of our power over nature, so too desisting from carrying an object acknowledges God's sovereignty over all affairs of society. Carrying from place to place is symbolic of the vast interchange of things and objects, and the whole gamut of human society and commerce. Carrying, or transferring material objects from one domain to another, is typical of the work which man pursues and attempts to achieve in society. Even the vast, complex world of social organisation – the home, the street, and public buildings – needs the sanctification and purpose which comes from the presence of God accompanying man in all his ways and deeds.

In modern times, as a rule of thumb, the labours prohibited on the Sabbath can be defined as follows: any activity of a creative or constructive nature which makes some significant change in our material environment. The rabbis define labour as the realisation of an intelligent purpose by practical skill. Thus, turning on any form of electrical appliance completes, or builds, a circuit, allowing the free flow of electrons, and is thus prohibited because of (a) building and (b) putting the final touches on a manufactured article. And significance is determined in relation to usefulness for human purposes.

But the important point is that by refraining once a week from creative labour, and dedicating that day to God, we come to acknowledge God's mastery over the earth, and our dependency upon Him for life and sustenance, without taxing the environment with our usual arrogance. Therefore, paradoxically, even recreational activities like gardening or playing music, in which man takes elements of God's created universe and brings improvement to them through exercising his higher creative talents, must be avoided if one seeks to become totally at one with creation.

There is no doubt that according to Jewish thought man is welcomed, even obliged, to join the Almighty as a junior partner in creation. For six days of every week, man is encouraged to use the raw materials which the Almighty created and enhances them by changing their form and position. Man *must* cut down trees and build a house, cook raw vegetables and make them edible, and experiment with medicines and cure disease. Although higher, the lesson the Sabbath teaches us is not meant to end all this.

Creation as an End not a Means

Once, Rabbi Samson Raphael Hirsch, who spent most of his time writing, educating and combating reformers of traditional Judaism, took off from his hectic schedule and left Frankfurt to see the Alps. When he returned his students asked him why he had gone. 'What will I say', he responded, 'if after my death, the Almighty asks me, as I stand before the heavenly throne, "Samson, did you see My Alps?"'

You may well ask, at this point in our discussion, how the Sabbath should be spent if it is not merely supposed to provide rest. The answer is that on that day, man must know his limitations. Man must seek to experience the majesty of creation in all its splendour and acknowledge the mastery of God. Rather than focus on what he might do with the components of the world, rather than indulge in the utilitarian aspects of life and how creation can benefit him and bring him pleasure, he must stop to experience the wonder of creation as an end in itself.

It is in this way that, each week, the Sabbath should infuse our society with the equality of mankind. By invading our institutions, the Sabbath reminds us that man is part of God's creation and His creation alone. The Bible commands that on the Sabbath day the bondsman and the maidservant must rest, just as their master rests. They are not the animated tools of their master to be used at will. Without it, human dignity would be difficult to imagine as people might be measured by productive capacity alone. It is, then, the great equalising factor, rendering all humanity as one.

Confounded by Leisure

One of the grandest indictments of modern-day men and women is that they have forgotten the value of peace. Even when we have a moment when we are not haunted by a sense of urgency to solve our daily problems we are at a loss with ourselves. We seem confounded by these all-too-scarce moments of leisure, ending up squandering whatever time we have for rest on trifling activities like watching television, sunbathing, reading trashy novels, and obsessively discussing our local sports teams. I believe that the greatest disease in modern society is not drugs, violence, or crime, but this boredom, this incapacity of ours to deal with leisure. And it will get worse. As Robert Lee wrote in *Religion and Leisure in America* about the centrality of free time to modern life, 'Literally a revolution has occurred – a turning around – for what was on the periphery is now at the heart of man's daily existence.' People today spend months and dedicate their highest creative energies toward planning their family holidays.

Leisure is as awkward to us now as it was to aristocratic society in ancient and more recent times. Commenting on the Southern California Research Council's (1962) prediction that by 1985 the typical worker in the USA would have the choice of a 25-week vacation, retirement at age 38, or a 22-hour work week, the orthodox Jewish thinker Rabbi Norman Lamm wrote that this is 'a truly frightening situation for the typical American who spends Sunday morning at church praying for eternity and the same rainy afternoon is at his wit's end because he cannot attend or watch the ball game on TV and has no idea what to do with his time!'

Like God, however, in our leisure, our passiveness, we show

our innermost selves. In what has become a famous state-ment, the Talmud declares that a man's character can be tested in three ways: *be'kiso, be'koso, u've'kaaso*, by his pocket – is he a miser or a spendthrift and on what does he spend his money; by his cup – how does he respond to the temptation of alcohol and what secrets emerge when he is intoxicated; and by his temper – can he control himself in the presence of provocation? There is a fourth test according to some: *af be'se-hoko*, by his 'play' – how does he use his leisure time?

One man who understood this exceptionally well was Victor Frankl, the wise Holocaust survivor who founded the therapeutic school of Logotherapy. In his brilliant *Man's Search for Meaning*, Frankl wrote that there is a 'kind of depression which afflicts people who become aware of the lack of content in their lives when the rush of the busy week is over and the void within themselves becomes manifest. Not a few cases of suicide can be traced back to this existen-tial vacuum. This is also true of the crises of pensioners and ageing people … [T]here are various masks and guises under which the existential vacuum appears. Sometimes the frus-trated will to meaning is vicariously compensated for by a will to power, including the most primitive form of the will to power, the will to money. In other cases, the place of frustrated will to meaning is taken by the will to pleasure. That is why existential frustration often eventuates in sexual compensation. We can observe, in such cases, that the sexual libido becomes rampant in the existential vacuum.'

Having grown up in Florida – America's largest retire-ment community – I can attest to the fact that so many of our dear elderly while away their retirement years playing cards and sitting idly in deck chairs in the sun, complaining that their dentures don't fit. The Lubavitcher Rebbe once said that retirement should be about putting on 'new tyres', and going stronger than ever before, rededicating our life to all that is important, at the stage of our life when we finally have the time to pursue it without the distraction of the urgent. The problem is that by the time we arrive at this special stage, it may be too late for modern man. In our old age, our deepest regrets will be that, now there is nothing urgent left, we cannot pursue the important because the opportunity has been squandered. The same parents who never had time for their children are confounded because the relationships with children and grand-children are non-existent. We wonder why our children don't visit us more.

The Abuse of Leisure

To the ancient rabbis, *sehok* represented the misuse of lei-sure. In one poignant example, the Talmudic sages ruled that the enforced idleness of a housewife, either because of an abundance of servants, or because her husband prevented her from working, was unacceptable. Rabbi Eliezer maintained that even if she had a hundred maids, she ought to do some work in or outside the household, 'for idleness leads to *zimah*, unchastity' and all boredom leads to sin. The rabbis went so far as to lay down that if the husband took a religious vow to abstain from benefiting from his wife's work, he must divorce her and pay her dowry and settlement. Summing up the negative consequences of inactivity, the rabbis declared, 'When there is nothing to do, you do what you ought not do.' How many delinquent teenagers would not have gone astray had they been totally absorbed into and animated by their studies?

Here we begin to see a deeper dimension of the Sabbath.

In the same way that the days of the week serve as the means for man to translate his creative potential into the actual, the Sabbath lends man the opportunity to master his side which is one with the universe. What the Bible requires from man on the Sabbath is that he avoids idleness. The difference between the prohibited labour and the recommended repose lies in the object of one's creative powers: oneself or one's environment; the inner world or the outer world. On the Sabbath, the Bible orders us to focus our creative powers on ourselves.

For orthodox Jews the way of resting on the Sabbath is devoting the day to the twin aims of phenomenal devotion in prayer, and the intellectual pursuit of Torah study. 'The Sabbaths were given to Israel in order that they might study Torah' (Jerusalem Talmud, Shab. 15:3), since intellectual development alone has never been enough for the Jew; it must be informed by a moral purpose. Jewish legend has it that it was Moses himself who instituted that a weekly portion of the fifty-three sections of the Bible be read in the synagogue, a custom that continues to this very day.

Serene Leisure

When Moses first encountered the Almighty in the wilderness, he saw a burning bush. He approached the bush to investigate the wondrous sight. The Bible says that at that point the Lord spoke to him from the bush, and the first thing He commanded Moses was to remove his shoes 'for the ground which you now stand on is holy.' Judaism is about teaching man to find the hallowed ground upon which no foot can trample.

Likewise, the Sabbath is meant to be about much more

than mere self-discovery. It is about the use of leisure for self-transformation. Instead of activity for the purpose of self-expression, it may require a certain type of personal, inner silence in which you make yourself available for a higher impression. In this higher form of rest – which necessitates prayer, contemplation, study, and every other tool of spiritual enrichment – man not only fulfils himself, but goes outside himself.

What the Sabbath teaches us, in particular, is to incorporate sanctity into other periods of our hectic week so that we may repress the impulse to let the urgent overtake the important. We must establish time spent with parents, spouse, siblings, and children as hallowed ground upon which no commercial or recreational pursuit may trespass. When Alexander the Great asked the great philosopher Diogenes whether he could do anything for him, the famed philosopher replied, 'Just stand out of my light.' This is one way of quietism in which the dizzying noise of the outside world is simply shut out. Indeed, the disciples of Rabbi Nahman of Bratslav used to set aside an hour a day known as the Dead Hour, in which all business would cease and nothing structured was permitted, allowing the repressed soul to come to the fore and be free.

Now, imagine if we could each make just two hours every day into a personal Sabbath. A mother sits to play with her children on a Wednesday evening. The phone rings, but she refuses to answer it, because the time she spends with her children is sacred, holy time. Her children are the Sabbath. Like her, treat your children as if there is nothing urgent that can ever supersede them. A man talks to his wife when he returns from work. Rather than have his wife wait as he sends one last fax from home, he understands that the time he spends working on his marriage is sacred time upon which there can be no intrusion. Just as if it were the actual Sabbath, he joins his wife because sending the fax is prohibited. Suddenly, he has made room in life for the important. He has liberated himself, and he is truly free.

3

The Jewish Nation

One of the saddest moments in the book of Genesis is the death of the matriarch Sarah. Throughout the book of Genesis, Abraham is portrayed as a loner. Armed with the courage of his convictions, he is prepared to risk social censure and estrangement in order to promote the truth of monotheism against the pagan mores of his time. His only and constant confidant is Sarah. Having lost her, he must now find a suitable burial ground. He does so in the form of the two-tiered cave belonging to Ephron the Hittite, telling the Hittites: 'I am both a *stranger* and a *resident* in your midst.'

This famous statement of the first Jew foreshadows the paradoxical nature of Jewish existence. Even today, Jews are equal citizens of their adopted lands. Jews in the United Kingdom are British, or American in the United States, or Bahamian in the Bahamas. But they are also distinctively recognised as Jews, part of another nation. They have a different New Year to the rest of the world, are circumcised, and don't celebrate some of the most important national holidays of their adopted lands, like Easter and Christmas.

How can they be both? Indeed, some Jews have, throughout the ages, tried to escape the torment of this dual identity by assimilating among Gentiles. Concerning such Jews, Rabbi Nahman of Bratslav gave a brilliant parable how a Jew cannot ever lose his Jewish identity. A king once had a son who thought he was a turkey. Ashamed, his father sought every wise man to cure the young prince, but to no avail. Stark naked and on all fours, the crown prince continued to roam the palace saying 'Gobble, gobble'. One day a rabbi came and claimed to be able to cure the prince. He removed his clothing and joined the prince, who was curious at the sight. 'Who are you?', asked the prince.

'Why me? I'm a bird.' 'That's amazing', said the prince. 'Why, I'm a bird too. I am so happy to have company.'

The next day, the rabbi forayed on the floor, but this time with his clothes on. 'I thought you were a bird,' inquired the prince. 'I am', responded the rabbi. But even birds can wear fine clothes.' 'You're right', said the prince, and put on his robes. Next, the rabbi appeared eating at a table. 'I thought you were a bird' said the prince. 'I am, but I don't see why birds shouldn't be cultured.' 'I agree', said the prince. And after a few weeks he was conducting himself with the finest etiquette, while still believing that he was a turkey. No matter what he thought, the prince could never change his essence. And neither can the Jew his Jewishness.

A People

In what sense, though, are the Jews a people within a people? Are they a race, like Black Africans and Native Americans? Or is their distinctiveness defined through their having common cultural practices? Are they a nation the way that the Irish are a nation, and do they identify through common history, a common land, and common cultural heritage? Or are they a nation defined by religious affiliation? Indeed, can they survive without their religion, and only through language, culture, and national will? And if Jews are defined primarily through having a common faith – that is they possess only a religious identity – then why is any notion of a national territory and national distinctiveness necessary to their religious identity? If they do need a common homeland called Israel, then why should religion be intrinsic to their identity? Why can't they be like the Kenyans, defined by geographical borders? Other questions are just as crucial. Can one only be born a Jew? Is a convert a full Jew? Are Jews distinct from, and therefore possibly better than, other nations or races?

Contrary to popular opinion, the Jews are not a race. The simple proof is that there are black Jews and white Jews, oriental Jews and Scandinavian Jews. Indeed, the Jewish nation comprises people of all races. While bound by a common faith, the Jews are not just united by a religion either. They constitute far more than a mere faith community. After all, there are religious Jews and secular Jews. Some claim to be atheists, while others are passionately orthodox believers in God. Yet nearly all Jews, regardless of degree of religious affiliation or belief in God, care deeply about their Jewishness. Isaac Bashevis Singer had a favourite yarn about this: 'I met a Jew who had grown up in a Yeshiva and knew large sections of the Talmud by heart. I met a Jew who was an atheist. I met a Jew who owned a large clothing store with hundreds of employees, and I met a Jew who was an ardent communist… It was all the same man.'

A classic case in point is that of Sigmund Freud, the founder of psychoanalysis. An affirmed atheist who embraced Austrian/German culture, he was still the proudest of Jews who on several occasions attempted to understand his latent Jewish identity. In his introduction to the Hebrew translation of *Totem and Taboo*, Freud wrote:

No reader of the Hebrew version of this book will find

it easy to put himself into the emotional position of an author who is ignorant of the language of Holy Writ, who is completely estranged from the religion of his fathers, as well as from every other religion, and who cannot take a share in nationalist ideals, but who has yet never repudiated his people, who feels that he is, in his essential nature, a Jew, and who has no desire to alter that nature. If the question were put to him: Since you have abandoned all these common characteristics of your countrymen, what is there left to you that is Jewish? He would reply: A very great deal, and probably its essence. He could not now express that essence clearly in words: But someday, no doubt, it will become accessible to the scientific mind.

In an address to the Bnei Brith Society, Freud, speaking as if he were a Jewish mystic, even defined Judaism as being 'not the faith, not even the national pride ... but many dark emotional powers, all the stronger the less they could be expressed in words, as well as the clear consciousness of an inner identity.'

A Covenant with God

How can this be? Why is it that even Jews who have forsaken every trace of religious or 'national' identity persistently refuse to relinquish the title 'Jew'? Throughout history, even the most secular of Jews have accepted and even died for their Jewishness rather than adopt another faith. Significantly, a large proportion of the many Jewish martyrs who refused to convert were non-observant Jews. A Catholic priest once described this phenomenon by claiming that 'the Jews are a people who are religious without even knowing it.' One of the biggest insults that a Jew may be given is being referred to as a non-Jew, a goy. Not because he is a racist. But because it denies an essential part of his nature.

What defines the Jews is that they are both a people, brothers and sisters of a single nation with a common ancestry, and a covenantal community bound by a divine covenant between their forebears and God. This covenant is binding on each and every Jew from now until the end of time. Having a natural affinity with Him, they share an innate orientation towards compassion for one's fellow man. As Elie Wiesel once said, 'A Jew can love God, or a Jew can hate God. But a Jew can never ignore God.' This innate spirituality and intuitive gravitation toward God is beautifully described in the Cabbalah as the natural gravitation of a flame to a torch. Put a small candle near a large flame, and the candle intuitively bends inward.

Consisting of the children of Abraham, Isaac, and Jacob, Sarah, Rebbeca, Rachel, and Leah, the Jewish people are a nation sharing a common ancestry, a common history and a common destiny. Being united by a common belief and common bond with their God, their people also include the righteous converts who have adopted and in turn been adopted by, the extended Jewish family. This image of the family is the most accurate definition. Even if you hate your father, you shall forever be his son. It is this that makes Judaism very different from being a Christian, which is an act of faith. Even one who was raised as a Christian will abandon this title if he rejects a belief in Christ. History, however, has shown time and time again that amidst the most strenuous efforts to blend in with the nations, the Jews always stick out in some way. God Himself seems to prevent the Jews from assimilating. As Job said, 'Thou dost pursue me like a lion.'

Converts

It is because of the covenant that in Judaism a convert to the faith is as Jewish as the prophet Moses, and there are several injunctions in the Torah forbidding the Jews from ever treating a convert as anything less than fully Jewish, or as a stranger. I have found that there is great apprehension among potential converts. They fear that they will always be treated as outsiders. This is certainly not the case. The only criterion for a convert to be fully embraced and accepted by the Jewish community is that their conversion is sincere and meets the following three requirements:

1. Converts must choose to join the Jewish nation for no other reason than their love for the God of Israel, His will as revealed in the Torah, and a desire to share the fate of the Jewish nation, for better or for worse. Conversions that are undertaken for ulterior motives – such as the leading contemporary reason, conversion in order to marry a Jew – are not valid. Ulterior motives impede the authenticity of the conversion. Certainly, a non-Jew can become interested in Judaism because they wish to accommodate their Jewish partner, but only insofar as their original desire to marry a Jew has now been superseded by a deep and honest appreciation for the sublimeness of the Jewish faith and their desire to lead a Jewish life. While a desire to marry a Jew can serve as the catalyst for conversion, it cannot be its sole motivating force.

2. The convert must be knowledgeable about the fundamentals of the faith, and undertake to carry out that knowledge in a life suffused with Jewish observance and commitment. Most rabbinical courts today who perform the conversions would insist on the candidate demonstrating a thorough knowledge and observance of the Sabbath and all the Jewish festivals, keeping a strictly kosher diet both inside and outside the home, and following the Jewish laws of family purity, which mandate a period of sexual abstinence in marriage for the five days of menstruation and seven days thereafter.

3. The candidate must go to the *mikveh*, the Jewish ritual pool of immersion. And if the candidate is a man, he must also be circumcised. If the candidate is already circumcised, then he need only have a drop of blood drawn in accordance with the circumcision ritual.

The Patriarchal and Sinaitic Covenant

The historical sequence of the development of the Jewish nation is that first they were a people, and only later were they given a religion and a covenant. All Jews are direct descendants of the original house of Abraham and are called Israelites as direct descendants of Jacob, to whom the Almighty gave the name Israel ('he who wrestles with God') after he battled with and prevailed against an angel. Later, after the dispersion of the ten lost tribes, the Israelite nation were referred to as Jews because the remainder of the Jewish nation – those that today form the bulk of the Jewish nation – nearly all stem from the tribe of Judah.

All of us, Jews and non-Jews, live two different, often

contradictory lives. There is the life we lead in the valley, and the life we live on the mountain. We are mostly in the valley, down in the dumps, harassed by the minutiae of life which drive us insane and cause us to miss the big picture. But then there are moments – however fleeting – when we are raised to the mountain. A wind of inspiration comes over us and we are lifted to the highest spiritual peaks. Contention and jealousy are drained from our heart and we experience the fraternity of the human family.

The greatness of life, however, we see from the great summits of inspiration which overtake us at times and energise us to complete our work. These are moments of inspiration when we are uplifted above the mundaneness of life and are shown a vision of what we all can rise to be. It was this spirit of inspiration that overtook one of David's greatest foes, Amasai, when he came over to David's camp: 'A feeling enfolded Amasai, the chief of the captains [and he said] "We are yours, David, on your side, son of Jesse; peace, peace be to you and peace to your helpers, for your God helps you." And David received them and put them at the head of the brigade.' (1 Chron. 12:18) At such moments, we are afforded a view of a higher reality in which all of creation reaches its fullest potential. Man can reach and touch the heavens and bring back of the heavenly bounty to earth. We realise that, although we must later return to earth, we can still conduct our lives according to how we viewed things 'on the mountain'.

For Jews, the Bible is that mountain. While the Bible consists of five books, the greatest source of inspiration lies undoubtedly in the book of Genesis and the book of Exodus. Here we not only read of great men and women at the dawn of history, rather, we read of the struggles of men and women just like you and me who rose to holiness by responding to a divine calling that entailed sacrifice. We learn of Abraham who was asked to leave behind everything he cherished – including his family and father's household – to find a higher destiny; Jacob and Joseph, who overcame feelings of vengeance to embrace the brothers who were guilty of attempted fratricide; and Moses who gave up the luxurious life of an Egyptian prince to redeem an enslaved nation.

We open up the pages of the Bible and we find living, breathing creatures who impart to us words of living inspiration. It is for this reason that God established two separate covenants between Himself and the Jewish people, something which is often overlooked. God established a Sinaitic covenant, which was formulated at Mount Sinai, and a patriarchal covenant which He made with Abraham, Isaac, and Jacob well before they had offspring.

Why two? The Sinaitic covenant tells the Jew what to do and what not to do, to act as a member of the covenantal community. It was established with the Jews for all eternity, and the Jews collectively committed themselves to adhering to all of God's commandments when they uttered the immortal words, 'We will do and we will listen.' The Jew must read in the Bible of Moses, whom God took up to a mountain for forty days and forty nights, teaching him His law and offering him a taste of paradise. Later, when God gives Moses commandments concerning the building of God's home on earth – the Tabernacle – He tells him to build His house 'according to the plan which I showed you on the mountain.' This covenant must be observed from a feeling of inspiration and redemption.

The patriarchal covenant addresses the 'I' awareness of the Jew, teaching him how to *experience* his Jewishness. It sensitises him in specifically Jewish ways. It expresses attitudes, ideals, and sentiments which still speak to us, guiding our feelings and consciousness rather than our physical acts, for we are duty-bound not only to act as Jews, but also to *feel* as Jews. In a word, it is the backdrop of the Sinaitic covenant. It is a covenant of inspiration and example, where the Sinaitic covenant is one of law and instruction.

The necessity for the patriarchal covenant is simple and straightforward: it imparts teachings to the Jewish people by example rather than by prescription. The Talmud says that the patriarchs did not die, since their children continue their legacy. Every time a Jew invites a guest home for the Sabbath – in the spirit of his forefather Abraham – he perpetuates Abraham's legacy and breathes new life into his immortal ancestor. In emulation of his open home, every Jewish couple marries under a wedding canopy symbolising a house with no doors. In the name of divine justice, Abraham interceded even for the wicked people of Sodom and Gomorrah and ever since then Jews have been at the forefront of fighting for social equality and justice. Sarah's wisdom regarding Ishmael drew divine approval, and ever since then Jews have been conditioned to allow their wives to make the most important decisions regarding positive and negative influences within the home.

Being in constant touch with the Bible is therefore an absolute prerequisite of the Jewish experience. Man is not only meant to respond to God as a disembodied voice. Rather, he is designed to acknowledge the God that lurks within, that He is an integral part of his very being. In studying and constantly hearing about the lives of our patriarchs and matriarchs, we absorb their values and nuances of feelings into our collective Jewish consciousness, until we are completely and positively influenced by their example.

The ancient rabbis therefore said, 'Every Jew should ask himself, "When shall my deeds be like those of Abraham, Isaac, and Jacob?"'

Circumcision and Holiness

As part of our discussion of Jewish identity, it becomes important to consider in greater detail the most significant identifying symbol for male Jews, which is also the very symbol of the covenant which God made with Abraham's offspring. Through extensive exposure to half-Jewish couples, I have discovered that a non-Jewish father usually has no objection to his children being raised as Jewish, except where circumcision is concerned. As one Gentile father said to me, 'My son was born perfect. So why do we need to cut him and tamper with his perfection?' Indeed, the story goes that Moses looked up to the heavens quizzically, and said, 'Now God, let me get this straight. The Arabs get all the oil, and we get to cut the tips of our *what*?'

What was the Creator thinking when he commanded so strange a practice? Although Jews overall remain highly devoted to the practice of circumcision – with a recent statistic showing that over 98 per cent of Jewish boys are circumcised – there is a sense of discomfort about the practice.

The first explanation we may offer for this most holy of Jewish rituals, is the recognition on the part of the Jew from the most tender of ages that everything he has belongs to God. This includes especially his body, but also his natural gifts, his aspirations and goals. The Jew must know that his sexual desire, representing the human life-force itself and the desire to perpetuate the species, is a means to a higher end.

Making us dependent on a soul-mate, sex causes us to draw a fragment of the divine into human flesh, and thus connects us with God.

There is however a deeper explanation. The ancient rabbis explain how in God there is an infinite and finite energy. When God created the world He used a special hylic substance which could assume any shape. This special substance derived from His infinite potential, which is endless and unlimited. Later, God shaped the world into its present form, thus giving definition and limits to creation. In man too there exists both an infinite and finite energy. Possessed of an infinite power for creativity, man is a creator. But he must also know when to stop creating. He must always be expansive and loving, but he must also learn when to put the brakes on. Thus, he must be compassionate and always show pity. But this must have its limits. The outcry against the cloning of humans demonstrates our innate understanding of the need to circumscribe our creative capacity. Man must show severity when the occasion calls for it, and a parent that cannot discipline their child does not truly love them.

The art of leading a fulfilling life is finding the fine balance between creativity and actualisation, between love and discipline, between indulgence and restraint. This is why God commanded that on the very reproductive organ itself – man's greatest symbol of his creative energy and his infinite capacity for Godly emulation – there must be a sign of God to teach man discipline. As the Psalmist chanted, 'I have always placed the Lord before me.'

What shakes and destroys our contemporary world is that people love but don't know when to stop loving, or how to love with discipline. A man marries but he does not learn the art of fidelity, or how to channel his love and make it potent by focusing it on just one woman, his wife. Humans, in contrast to animals, are the creatures who can fundamentally control, uplift, and even reverse their natures. Note that the very first commandment given to Adam and Eve in the Garden of Eden was a negative prohibition. They were ordered not to partake of the fruit of the tree of knowledge of good and evil. They were taught that the essence of being distinguished from an animal is an ability at times to suppress material indulgence and sensual pursuits.

In Judaism, the meaning of holiness is separateness. If no one remembers your birthday, or a couple treats their anniversary like any other day, it can hardly be said to have been special. God is holy because He is aloof, distinct, and removed from the realm of man. A man becomes holy when he refuses to be carried away with social trends that run contrary to the divine will. Circumcision, therefore, is holy precisely because it makes the Jew distinct. It consecrates his life and procreative capacity to a higher purpose, so that he is not ruled by his passions. While others may engage in sex for the selfish purpose of sensual gratification only and through hormonal compulsion, he engages in intimate human contact in order to become one flesh with his married partner, and to draw new fragments of the divine being into an earthly body. By bringing discipline to the realm of the animal within us, man becomes sanctified within his own distinct and unique humanity.

The Covenant and Truth

Though Judaism does make room for converts, it does not encourage conversion. How are its covenants consistent with other faiths and even atheism? I have had many public debates with secular humanists and confirmed atheists. In each a similar argument against religion has been proposed. Every year the L'Chaim Society hosts a 'Science versus Religion' debate, and very often the leader of the science team is one of the world's most famous atheists and exponents of Darwinism, Richard Dawkins, Oxford Professor of the Public Understanding of Science. Among Richard Dawkins's strongest criticisms of religion in these debates is the simple fact that so many contradictory religions claim to have the truth. Likewise, a friend of mine who is the religious correspondent for a national newspaper said to me that what most undermines religion is the fact that they fight with and denounce each other – where does that leave Godliness?

Judaism is unique among the world's religions in that it claims no copyright on, or exclusivity to, truth. As such, it does not suffer from the defect of denouncing other faiths as misguided or heretical. No other religion has been so adamant about the fact that it bears no copyright on truth as Judaism. There are many paths to the one God, and Judaism is *a* path, not *the* path. There is no need for a non-Jew to become Jewish in order to be close to God or to receive divine rewards. Indeed, the world to come will be inherited by all the righteous of the world, rather than the Jews alone.

Judaism is a science of living by which the Jew – with his unique spiritual constitution – can actualise his fullest human potential. The Jewish people were given a special mission in this world, which was to educate and teach the other nations of the world to love God, pursue justice, and spread compassion on the earth. Judaism accomplishes these goals through an emphasis on law as the cornerstone of living. That is not to say that Judaism has nothing to learn from Christian love or Muslim passion. On the contrary, the fact that each of the great monotheistic faiths shines in one important category just shows how much they can learn from one another.

Believing that there are a series of truths possessed by each nation, Judaism holds that when amalgamated, these together will create *the* truth. So long as any religion leads to humility and worship of the one God, as well as including passionate religious rituals which lead to compassion and loving kindness, then it has created a legitimate path to the God of the universe. For truth is like a giant jigsaw puzzle that becomes more and more complete with more and more pieces added. Each nation and monotheistic religion has been given one huge chunk of truth which becomes completely authentic only when amalgamated with all the others. Jews, Christians, and Muslims have so much to learn from each other if they would only just stop and listen.

Take the sexes. The world is possessed of masculine and feminine virtues. But it would be a mistake for either gender to assume their superiority over the other by virtue of their inherent gifts. On the contrary, femininity is truth for a woman and best accords with her personality and biological constitution. Masculinity is true for a man, and if a man were to lead a completely feminine life, it would not accord with his deepest self. But left alone, neither of these truths is capable of generating life and each is profoundly incomplete without the other. Similarly, for a man to want to have a baby, or for a woman to want to grow a beard, is a case of mistaken potential and a misguided identity. What is needed is for each to accept their individual identity amidst a commitment toward mutually enriching the other through working together.

The same is not true, however – and here I apologise if I

sound intolerant – of those religions which are polytheistic in nature. The one great truth of the world is the one true God. And any religion whose destination is not God is a false doctrine that cannot enrich the monotheistic believer. Rather than furthering the unity of all mankind and man's inner forces, these religions strengthen the fragmentation caused by competing forces that exist in our world. This is not to say that there is not much good in these religions. It just means that their fundamental premise is false. Religions that lead to no God, or to many gods, ultimately lead back into darkness, steering us away from the truth.

The manner in which the Almighty created us is the way in which He wishes for us to develop our fullest spiritual and material potential. Judaism does not believe that converts upgrade their existence by becoming Jewish, and indeed the ancient rabbis declare that the righteous Gentile, who leads a moral and ethical life, has an equal share in the immortal hereafter. As early as 900 years ago, Maimonides wrote that non-Jews who live by the seven Noachide commandments, would inherit the same place in heaven as a Jew and can be considered to be as holy as the Jewish high priest. Judaism, therefore, discourages conversion. This is not because it is an elite club that does not allow new members. Rather, Judaism sees all people as being inherently holy and Godly, just the way they are born. They are perfect the way God made them. Jews are not closer to God than Gentiles.

Tolerance is an important lesson that Judaism can teach all world religions. Although being the world's oldest mono-theistic faith, the Jews have never insisted that their beliefs are superior to others. Neither have the Jews ever persecuted another nation for not adopting Judaism. Coercion is as foreign to Judaism as Christmas. A close and very religious friend of mine adopted a Christian girl at the age of twelve whose parents were killed in a car crash. Although the girl grew up in a devoutly religious Jewish home, her foster parents insisted that she be raised a Christian, which is what her parents would have wanted. The girl went on to marry a vicar, and is a devout Christian until this day, although always being treated as an equal member of an orthodox Jewish family, like any other of the family's biological children. Those who suggest that the Jewish State of Israel treats its Arab citizens as second-rate citizens are misguided. What divides the Israelis and the Palestinians is a geo-political dispute rather than any theological programme of subordination. Judaism does not allow any discrimination against any law-abiding minority.

The rabbis of the Talmud also taught 'Do not despise any man' (Avos 4:3). Likewise they declared, 'Even a Gentile who studies God's law is equal to a High Priest.' These rabbis saw God's salvation freely available to all men. Contrast this with the terrible sentence proclaimed in the name of Jesus (John 15:6) 'He who does not abide in me is thrown away like a withered branch. Such withered branches are gathered together, cast into the fire and burned.' This intolerant statement was later used by the Catholic Church to justify their practice of burning non-believers at the stake.

Many people have asked why it is that Judaism consists of 613 commandments, while the law given to the rest of mankind, the Noachide covenant – consisting of only seven commandments, among which are prohibitions against idolatry, blasphemy, murder, theft, cruel treatment of animals, sexual immorality, and the positive commandment to uphold justice – is so much less in number. If Judaism indeed believes in the equality of all mankind, then why are there different, unequal ways of serving God? The answer lies in the covenant. As Jews are meant to spread the light of God and ethical monotheism without conversion of Gentiles, they require a higher degree of spiritual armoury to offset the often hostile environments into which they are immersed. Imagine a home during winter. In order for the rooms of the house to remain a comfortable 70 degrees, the boiler, from which the heat is generated, must be 300 degrees. The same is true of the Jews.

The Jewish attitude toward non-Jews is most eloquently expressed in King Solomon's prayer, where he says, 'When a stranger, who is not of Your people Israel, but comes from a distant land … turns in prayer toward this Temple, then listen to his prayers' (1 Kings 8:41-43). Indeed, King David proclaims in the book of Psalms, 'God is good to all, and His love extends over all His works.' Indeed, two thousand years ago the ancient rabbis legislated that a Jew is obligated to assist a needy Gentile as much as any Jew: 'We are obliged to feed the Gentile poor in exactly the same manner as we feed the Jewish poor' (Gittin 61a).

4

The Messiah

Long ago in the Jewish *shtetles* of Eastern Europe, there lived a man who could not support his family but refused to be a ward of the community. Fearing that his children would starve, the elders of the community created a post for him that even he could not fail. They made him Chief Messiah Watcher. With great pride, he took up his post at the gates of the city. Day in and day out he sat there, waiting to herald to his Jewish brethren the imminence of redemption.

One day his brother came to visit him and asked, 'What are you doing sitting like a baboon at the gates of the city doing nothing?'

'Nothing!' the Chief Messiah Watcher replied indignantly. 'You say, I'm doing nothing? I'll have you know that I have been given the most important task in the community. I am the official Messiah Watcher.'

His brother shook his head. 'You imbecile. Don't you realise that they are just making fun of you?'

'Well, I guess you're right', the Chief Messiah Watcher agreed. 'But at least it's a steady job.'

Action through Hope

Aside from the concept of God Himself, there is no more influential or exciting idea in Judaism than that of the Messiah. The Jewish idea of a righteous figure who will one day inspire mankind to redemption offered the world an entirely new direction from other cultures or religions. Indeed, all of Judaism may be said to be an attempt at perfecting man and the world, the culmination of which will take place when the final touches are added by God Himself. So central is Messianism that Maimonides listed the belief in the coming of the Messiah as the penultimate principle of his thirteen articles of Jewish faith and the culmination of the first eleven.

Why was the idea of a Messiah so revolutionary? For one, it contrasted sharply with the cyclical view of history that dominated the ancient world. Babylon offered a stagnating view of the world in which history was the story of man's vacillation between two opposing forces. And even the ancient Greeks wrote of the power of fate and were obsessed with the idea that all hope was futile since man could not overcome predetermined destiny. The essence of all their great tragedies is a hero or heroine, trapped in a catch-22, who is ultimately doomed to oblivion because he or she cannot overcome the power of fate. The most depressing aspect of a cyclical view is that nothing really can get better. From the Hindu perspective, for example, there are the seven days and seven nights of Krishna. Everything which is created is destined to be destroyed. Every human story has been lived once before in the past and every human soul is a repeat of an earlier existence. So why establish hospitals or social-welfare services when, in the final analysis, the effort is for naught?

For me, mornings are the worst part of the day. I wake up more than a little disillusioned with my inability to achieve all my goals. I am then reminded of King David leaping out of bed like a predator. Unstoppable, he wrote the moving prayer: 'Awake, my soul! Awake, O harp and lyre! I will awake the dawn' (Psalms 57:8). This is the essence of Judaism. Because of their belief in the Messiah, the Jewish people developed a dazzlingly optimistic view that confirmed the perspective of man as master of his own destiny. It told them that positive human action would always be cumulative and would lead to a more highly developed and just society. Rather than feeling abandoned in moments of misfortune, the concept of a linear history leading to salvation allowed them to consider even the greatest tragedies as just anomalies or upsets along the road. Analogous to a physics student being given enormously complex mathematical equations, the Jews know that there is a Professor who has the answers and who is willing to assist if they make an effort.

This jubilant view of history and man's place in it has found a deep resonance in the Western world, where it drives us on to advance the perfection of our society and environment. What else inspired the nations of the world to come together in San Francisco in April 1945 to establish the United Nations? The nations that convened the conference were still in the midst of fighting the worst war the world had ever seen, resulting in the deaths of millions of soldiers and civilians. Not long before this date, historians, politicians and philosophers were convinced that war is endemic to mankind. Social Darwinism, for example, claimed that civilisations would always battle against one another in their struggle for limited resources. Only through hope could they now aim to establish global co-operation and an end to national hostilities. Eloquently, a Biblical verse etched on the Wall of Peace standing in the Plaza of Nations at UN Headquarters in New York recites their hopes in the face of all this evil: 'Swords shall be beaten into ploughshares ... Nation shall not lift up sword against nation, neither shall they learn war anymore' (Isa. 2:4).

God and History

Nonetheless, many might still wonder why the Messianic belief has remained a core teaching of Judaism. Why wasn't it relegated to a less obvious role? As mentioned at the beginning of the book, even the best ideas are subject to fashion as much as anything else. With a bad press it isn't hard for any of them to fail. So, it seems a fair question to ask why this particular belief did not flounder in Judaism's three-thousand year history, whereas the conceptions of other religions have been modified or, worse, have disappeared without a trace.

The answer lies in Judaism's approach to history. According to secular history every event is brought about by a preceding cause and history develops mechanically. Origins determine events and the present is merely one of a number of possible precipitations of the past. Hence, the future has many causes. Jewish history is different. Ultimately, it is not pushed by antecedent causes, for all of history converges on the righteous future heralded by the Messiah. Rabbi Joseph Soloveitchik put this most succinctly in *Man of Faith in the Modern World*: 'While universal [non-Jewish] history is governed by causality, by what preceded, covenantal [Jewish] history is shaped by destiny, by a goal set in the future'! What determines Jewish historical experience, therefore, is not the point of departure of events, but their destination. The engine of history is tomorrow's promise rather than yesterday's events.

Messianism is indestructible because it is a direct consequence of the Jewish concept of the one God. A Jew feels in his bones that His being, not fractious causality, runs the motor of history. And as its destination He cannot be doubted. Thus, Rabbi Yehuda Lowe of Prague, famed as the Maharal who built the Golem, wrote: 'The essential function of the Messiah will consist of uniting and perfecting all, so that this will be truly one world' (q BWC, 176). Or, in the more ancient words of the prophet Zechariah: 'The Lord shall be king over all the earth; in that day shall the Lord be One and His Name One' (Zech. 14:9).

The Messiah

Obviously, essential to the Messianic age is the Messiah himself, a human leader who will spur humanity to perfect his world. Ever since the great prophet Moses led the Jewish people from slavery in Egypt to the borders of the land of Israel, such a person has been central to the Jewish nation. As a result, many great men and women have left their mark on Judaism in the course of history. Indeed, there is a feeling among those who are conversant with the classic Jewish texts – the Bible, the prophets, and the Talmud – that these giants of Jewish history are in a sense alive even today. Jewish thinking remains profoundly influenced not just by, for example, the teachings of Moses, but also by his personality and charisma in so far as we can still sense them across the centuries.

Why is this human leadership so central? Why can't we leave matters to social currents and other forms of direction? Since the purpose of religion is to change the individual, it would seem far more desirable to have society give rise to righteousness of its own accord, without the external stimulus of men and women in positions of power. As we know so well, leadership lends itself to tyranny and can induce a sense of dependence of the populace on the leader, rather than have them learn to fend for themselves. Moses himself complained of this development to the Almighty. 'Did I conceive all this people? Did I give birth to them, that you should say to me, "Carry them in your bosom, as a nurse carries a sucking child", to the land that you promised on oath to their ancestors?' (Numbers 11:12).

The answer is that Judaism believes that there is an essential need for someone who serves as the living embodiment of Jewish teachings. One of the great problems with ideals is that often they do not work in practice. The Talmud says that just before a thief breaks into a home to steal its contents, he first pauses for a moment prior to the crime, lifts his eyes heavenward, and offers a prayer to the Almighty that he should not be caught. In other words, faith doesn't by itself shape or affect our actions. We may still err even with the strongest faith.

A leader is someone who translates ideology into reality within his own person. Certainly, a child may be inspired by glorious stories of giants like Abraham, who defended even the people of Sodom and Gomorrah when God sought to destroy them. We may read in the Bible moving accounts of how Moses was the most humble man that ever lived. We may further hear about the great Jewish masters in recent history, such as Don Isaac Abravanel who chose to share the exile of his Jewish brethren in Portugal rather than lead the most comfortable life in Spain as finance minister to Ferdinand and Isabella. But when there is a man or woman who lives in your time, with whom you are acquainted, who faces the same challenges as you do, who lives up to all these lofty ideals, you can no longer dismiss great virtue as being outside your own personal reach.

The Talmud relates that when a poor man dies, his soul rises before the angels who ask him whether he dedicated his life to the study and observance of God's commandments. The poor man answers, 'Me, why I couldn't. I was too poor.' The angels then ask him, 'Were you poorer than the great sage Hillel? Hillel was so poor that he had to climb in the snow to the rooftop of the study hall where Shmaya and Avtalyon were teaching, because he did not possess even the few dinar it took to gain entry.' To the rich man who complains that he had too many responsibilities to find any time for worthwhile pursuits, the angels say, 'Were you richer than the great Rabbi Eliezer ben Hyracanus, who owned a fleet of hundreds of vessels, and yet still found the time to become one of the greatest scholars of his generation?'

Moses and the Messiah

Once in France, I chanced upon the French handicapped skiing championships. There was a young girl competing in a ski wheelchair with numbers on her front and back. Her number was about to be called and she was practising with her mother on a small slope. She kept falling over and could not get up. On the third attempt to rise, she burst into tears and called for her mother to lift her up. Her mother refused. 'But I can't move my feet', she sobbed. 'But look, you can move your arms,' was her mother's response. 'Try and pick yourself up.'

There are two ways of helping people. The first way is to pull them out of trouble, shield them from sorrow. No doubt, this is a righteous action. But the drawback is that it creates a lasting dependency. A far better method is to impart to the individual the capacity to save themselves. Instead of creating a dependency, this method sets off a chain reaction of empowerment in which one person inspires another to bring about redemption by their own personal devices.

The first appointed leader of the Jewish people was Moses and the last will be the Messiah himself. Contrasting the two will clarify this distinction and show how the Messiah will be different. The name of Moses means to 'draw', to 'cull' or to 'extract'. Judaism believes that an individual's name is not coincidental but is rather a mystical entity which contains the essence of that individual's nature, and helps explain the inner working of their destiny. In this spirit the Zohar states that every time parents name a child, they are inspired by prophecy. There is a spiritual connection between the name of an individual and his soul. Rabbi Isaac Luria, the greatest Jewish mystic of all time, wrote that the nature and behaviour of a person, whether good or bad, can be found by analysing his name.

Moses the leader drew forth of himself and his unparalleled stature to give to the Jewish people who were spiritually bereft. While Moses was a spiritual giant, the Jews were spiritually in their infancy. Like a nursemaid, Moses took of his own milk and gave it to the Jewish people. It was his own spiritual greatness which made the Jewish people worthy. Time and time again, the Almighty agreed to spare the rebellious nation of Israel for Moses's sake.

Moses was the redeemer who brought the Torah down from Sinai, drawing the Torah down from the heavens. It was a feat accomplished entirely through him. He then gave the Torah as a gift to the Jewish people. It had to be a gift because they themselves were undeserving of it. Having just been slaves in Egypt who had almost completely assimilated into Egyptian culture, they were not intellectually, emotionally, or spiritually prepared for such intimate divine communion.

So began a process of dependency that existed between Moses and the Jewish people for the entire forty years in the desert. Moses's leadership was in effect the leadership of the elite, the triumph of aristocracy. He was acknowledged by all as the greatest of the Jews. But his greatness made everyone around him feel dependent. The Jews needed Moses in the wilderness. Everything from their food to their clothes rained down in miraculous manner in the merit of the great lawgiver. The Jews needed to do nothing save sit back and enjoy the ride. Moses would take care of everything.

Judaism never conceived of a Christian Jesus-like figure who would come along and redeem mankind of their iniquity irrespective of their actions. The Jewish Messiah is not a divine figure or the son of a deity. He will simply be someone who distinguishes himself by an ability to bring out the good in vast numbers of people. Using his charisma and piety, he will spur mankind on to redeem themselves. This idea is best expressed in the Jewish tradition that the name of the Messiah will be Menachem, which means 'Comforter'. The name Menachem, therefore, teaches that the Messiah will bring redemption by way of being a comforter rather than a redeemer.

In contemporary terms, Moses resembled a philanthropist. He was like a government of the developed world who comes to the Third World with foreign aid. The act is selfless and humanitarian. But it is also a condescending action from strong to weak, from the haves to the have-nots. Because of this dependent model of leadership, Moses was able to take the Jews out of Egypt, but he could not bring them into the promised land. Once there, the Jews would have to fend for themselves and create an independent commonwealth. They would have to fight against their enemies and displace nations who were already in the land.

A comforter will act in an entirely different way. Imagine someone who, after years of toil, loses his business and goes bankrupt. They sit at home and sulk. Unlike Moses, the comforter will not offer them any money. Nor does he offer them a good, high-paying job. Rather, he makes the businessman focus on what he already has. He says to him 'You may have lost a lot, but just think of what you still have. You have your health, a wife, children, and most of all, you have the potential to rebuild yourself. If you made it to the top one time, you can do it again.' The comforter harnesses one's inner gifts and inspires self-redemption.

Abraham Lincoln and Martin Luther King

In modern history we see these two types of leadership too and how one precedes the other historically. Abraham Lincoln was a redeemer to the black slaves of America who gave to them like Moses. His message to American black slaves was, 'Stand by and I will free you. Our armies will liberate you.' He brought them liberty and the promise of a better life.

But granting them their external freedom was no guarantee that they would gain *internal* freedom, the belief that they didn't need the white man for a glorious black future. Therefore, even after the freeing of the slaves, blacks in America suffered continued racism and exclusion from opportunity. The freeing of the slaves ultimately led to thousands of disaffected and angry black youths who shouted that they were tired of whites promising them everything and giving them nothing. They acknowledged that much of their freedom was brought about through whites, but to an extent this just made matters worse. It led to a feeling of inferiority and degradation.

Now, contrast Lincoln's actions with those of the Rev. Martin Luther King Jr. His whole mission to black America was to teach them how they should not be, and are not, reliant on an outside redeemer. King nurtured black pride which led black America to believe in and redeem *themselves*, a revolution which carries on until this very day.

Accepting Responsibility

Ironically, Messianic pretensions have been the scourge of the Jewish people at times when the concept wasn't understood properly. The rejection of the Messiahship of Jesus has led to the persecution of Jews throughout the ages. And there have been false Messiahs like Shabbatai Zevi, the sixteenth-century Messianic pretender from Izmir, Turkey. Jews had already sold their property in anticipation of the final redemption when they discovered that the man in whom they had placed all their hopes had become an apostate to Islam. Similarly, Moses of Crete, promising the Jews that the millennium was at hand, encouraged his many thousands of Jewish followers to jump into the sea which he promised to part.

Until the righteous redeemer finally arrives, it is, therefore, of immense importance that all of us nurture the Messiah in our hearts. Each of us is born with the deep-seated conviction that we are special. Social anthropologists note common fantasies which many children have. One of the most recurrent is a belief that the whole world was made for them and revolves around them. Every American child believes that he or she can grow up to be President. The same must be true for the Messiah. Every Jewish child should grow up believing that perhaps it is him or her. Maybe, just maybe, he himself is the ancient Jewish redeemer that has been promised by God and awaited by the Jews for so many thousands of years.

Messianism, ultimately, is the call to each and every one of us to become a Messiah. Indeed, we all feel that if we didn't wake up tomorrow morning, the world would miss something irreplaceable. Nine hundred years ago, Maimonides wrote that every individual has the capacity to comfort and redeem. He wrote: 'One must always see the world as being perfectly balanced between good and evil. Thus, if a single individual does even one good deed, they tip the earth's balance into righteousness and redemption.'

The man who will ultimately be the Messiah is not someone who will claim to have all the answers. Nor will he disown those who claim to have other solutions. Instead, he will harness the unique aspect of every contributor so that the world becomes more complete than ever before – to the point where the critical mass of goodness is reached, and the hidden light of creation is finally manifest for all to see.

Though there will be a scion of the House of David who will usher in a new era of peace, the long-awaited Messiah, even today all of us must strive to be 'little Messiahs' who redeem our corner of the earth. Each of us has a portion in the world that only we can comfort and unite with the rest of creation. To the young child waiting at home for his father to arrive from work, that man is the Messiah. He is the person who plays with the child and makes him feel loved. No one else can take his place. To a man broken by the pain of the world, his wife is the Messiah, who makes him feel indispensable, even when his employers make him redundant. To the woman who has always dreamed of finding love and fulfilment, the man who comes home to her every night and tells her that she is the most special person on the planet is the Messiah. To the friend who has just broken up from a relationship and desperately seeks someone to talk to, you are the Messiah.

In thinking that we are the Messiah, we will try to improve the lot of our fellow man today. We will never allow an opportunity to feed the hungry, comfort the bereaved, uplift the helpless, and inspire the young, to pass us by. In fact, if we do not believe that we are the Messiah, if we think that so grand a title is completely outside our reach, we will have excused ourselves from the goodness that we can impart to the world.

Emulation, Not Admiration

In *The Day America Told the Truth*, thousands of Americans interviewed agreed that there was 'a general decline in moral and ethical standards'. The majority of people interviewed attributed this to a dearth of leadership. There was no longer anyone to look up to. It is true for all of us. Gone from the landscape are the charismatic leaders of just a generation ago, the Churchills, the Roosevelts, the De Gaulles. What a difference it would make if our leaders were both compassionate, intent on making things better, and at the same time a *tzaddik* (a righteous man whose righteousness is recognised by Jew and non-Jew alike)! Does this mean that our leaders should be perfect?

According to Judaism, leaders need not be faultless. It

distinguishes between hypocrisy and inconsistency. The Bible records the many mistakes of its greatest heroes. According to the rabbis, Moses was the supreme apostle of truth, even to the detriment of his own popularity with the Israelites. He would call them as he saw them, and was under no circumstances prepared to compromise. 'Moses is true and his Torah is true.' As a result, the Bible indicates, Aaron, who pursued love and compassion over and above truth and justice, was far more popular. The rabbis of the Talmud declared that Aaron even found it acceptable to conceal or modify the truth in order to promote peace. Thus, in counselling sessions within troubled marriages, he would often give a skewed and favourable account to husbands and wives who in private had really been critical of each other. The Bible records: 'When all the congregation saw that Aaron had died, *all* the house of Israel mourned for Aaron thirty days' (Num 20:29 NRSV). For Moses, however, it says that only the men mourned: 'The Israelites wept for Moses in the plains of Moab thirty days; then the period of mourning for Moses was ended' (Deut. 34:8 NRSV).

If we are truly honest, we recognise that we all have a tendency to distinguish ourselves from great men and women, dismissing them as saints. By depicting them as angelic figures we remove them from earthly reality. 'Of course', we say, 'Abraham was able to defy the entire pagan world and teach the earth's inhabitants about God. After all, he was a saint! But me? I'm just an ordinary person. I don't think I can do what they did. It takes such courage.'

This delusion Judaism is at pains to avoid. As opposed to the New Testament, it goes out of its way to demonstrate the character *and* flaws of its great heroes. It teaches us in this way that great leaders are ordinary mortals. They are born as man and die as man. But, in between those two events, they lead lives dedicated to the highest ideals and most noble goals. They attempt to leave the earth in a far more Godly fashion than how they found it, despite a human propensity to do otherwise. Judaism gears everything towards the message 'And now it is time for you to do the same.'

Saints and the Clergy

I once published an essay which asked the question why we can never be totally in love, why it is that even after marriage we are still attracted to strangers. I went on to explain that it is this attraction to others which forces us to constantly choose our spouse anew thereby guaranteeing that the marriage always remains fresh and exciting. An angry rabbinic colleague called me up shortly afterwards and said that in this essay I sound like the gynaecologist who admits to being aroused by his patients!

'But was there anything untrue about the question I put?', I asked him. And his response was: 'It's certainly not true in my case. My wife is the only woman to whom I am attracted. To me any other woman is just the same as a block of wood.' Now, he might have been telling the truth. But as another colleague with whom I discussed the issue remarked, he might also be a very bad carpenter!

Until the Messiah arrives, the people whom we have to lead us toward ever higher rungs of the spiritual ladder are rabbis, priests, imams, and other clerics. The mere fact that rabbis feel the need to deny for themselves what to everyone is human is puzzling. Of course clerics have egos, and of course they have libidos. Clerics are no different to other people. They have the same natures, the same desires, and the same materialistic orientation. But what should distinguish them from the rest of their communities is not their in-born nature, but rather what they do with that nature; to what use it is employed.

The boy who dreams of being a priest one day is no less ego-driven than the boy who dreams of being chairman of IBM. Both wish to be recognised. The difference, however, lies in the fact that the one who wishes to head IBM only thinks about how he can use his ambition to benefit himself, while the one who wants to be a cleric wants to use his nature to benefit other people. He doesn't want to be a loser who serves God. He wants to be a winner who earns the respect of his peers by aiding humanity. A cleric has the same blood and the same ambitions as his congregants; the only real difference between them lies in the fact that the cleric has taken upon himself the commitment to try and employ his humanity in the service of a cause that is greater than himself.

When people claim that they receive little or no inspiration from their rabbis these days, they are no doubt right in assuming there exists a general failure in the way clergy connect with their congregants. But people today do seem to expect the impossible from their clerics. In an English newspaper article, I was quoted as saying 'People tell me that I am ego-driven. I take that as a compliment. By saying that clerics can have no ego, you end up getting people that are passive and even mediocre becoming rabbis and priests.' Little did I know that this harmless quote would cause one woman in Glasgow to order me to leave the British Isles and return to America. 'You're nothing but a braggart,' she said, 'You're not a real rabbi.' But does anyone know of even one rabbi who doesn't occasionally boast! And is it even in our interest to expect that a rabbi has mastered every one of his foibles?

Unrealistic expectations for clerics have led to standards of behaviour well above those of ordinary mortals. Congregants want their leaders at once to be angelic and spiritual, but they also want them to be fully human. Clerics have to have an understanding of human dilemmas so that they can offer advice. But they are not permitted to experience the same dilemmas themselves. For instance, they have to be able to counsel people out of depression, but they are never allowed to be depressed themselves. All these unrealistic expectations of rabbis and ministers create an environment where they are forced to become liars. If they tell the truth, their reputations will be in tatters. If they admit to the same cravings and yearnings as lesser mortals, their communities will stop respecting them.

One of the things religion today is suffering from is its dissuasion of ambitious people to enter its ranks in the first place. Let me offer you this challenge: can you name even one person, aside from Mother Teresa, who is world-famous for being nice? I don't mean someone who is famous for a different reason, but decides to use his office for good things, like Jimmy Carter who is far better at being a humanitarian than he was at being President of the United States. I just mean someone who is famous for their acts of kindness and compassion on behalf of the people around them.

It is a shame that so many potentially good people choose to go into corporate finance or politics rather than humanitarian work and religion because they feel that these latter two are incompatible with personal ambition. All the talented and ambitious people chase money and power because they mistakenly believe that religion is about sacrifice and fighting one's nature rather than about personal development and enhancement of self with a view toward the benefit of others; channelling all one's ambitions for good and positive things. They see their rabbis and priests as so much less accomplished than they. So why should they listen to anyone who is one step below on the ladder of life?

The real message of religion is that every single one of us is born with an innate nature, which we should not subvert, but channel in the right direction. Don't fight your nature. Rather develop it! You're an ambitious person, you want to have your name up in lights? No problem! Do thousands of good deeds on behalf of thousands of people, and you will be loved and famous. Use your human nature to other people's advantage. Never stamp it out. According to Judaism, everything in life is neutral. It is the use to which it is put that matters. Passion can be phenomenal. It's the direction that makes it either a good thing, or a rotten thing.

5

Law

The L'Chaim Society was founded on the principle that Judaism can compete and win in the marketplace of ideas. For this reason, we are prepared to host virtually any speaker on virtually any subject. We were especially proud to host the celebrated Jewish playwright, Peter Shaffer, of *Amadeus* fame, who spoke under our auspices on the occasion of an Oxford student production of his play, *Yonadav*. In his remarks, Shaffer, like many Jewish intellectuals, contrasted 'the vengeful and capricious' God of the Old Testament, with the 'humanitarian and ethical' teachings in the New Testament. He spoke of the barbarity of the Old Testament and how it was all about law. Many contrast this with the Christian Bible, which is all about love.

Shaffer's sentiment is one that I have heard expressed many times. Not long ago, in fact, a bright Oxford student walked into my office holding a book 'You just have to read this book, Shmuley. It's the most beautiful book about God.' The book in question claimed to be a direct prophetic dialogue with God. And in its quest for God, it said, 'ministers, rabbis, Priests ... even the Bible ... are not authoritative sources. Then what is? Listen to your feelings. Listen to your highest thoughts. Listen to your experience. Whenever any of these differ from what you've been told by your teachers, or read in your books, forget the words. Words are the least reliable purveyor of Truth.'

It is undeniable that Judaism champions law above love, practice above faith, and religious service above theology and dogma. Still, Judaism maintains these beliefs whole-heartedly. In the words of the Jewish sages, 'He who is kind to those who are cruel will end up being cruel to those who are kind.' But there is no doubt that they are difficult ideas to communicate. People want a religion that makes them feel wonderful and all comfortable. Judaism, with its strong emphasis on law, is not always suited to this desire.

Law and Love

This view, like the comparisons between Jesus's magnanimous 'turn the other cheek' teaching versus the Hebrew Bible's 'eye for an eye' law (which has, in fact, always been interpreted in Judaism to mean financial compensation for an eye), actually goes back to the very origins of Christianity, in which St Paul in his letters continually upbraids Judaism for being weighed down by law at the expense of love.

The two operative words in Christianity are faith and love, designed to undermine and replace the two central words in Judaism, law and commandment. 'For sin will have no dominion over you, since you are not under law but under grace' (Rom. 6:14); and again, 'But now we are discharged from the law, dead to that which held us captive, so that we are slaves not under the old written code but in the new life of the Spirit' (Rom. 7:6).

A more modern case in point is that of the celebrated English man of letters, Sir Edmund Gosse. Sir Edmund wrote in his autobiography that when his father was teaching him the book of Hebrews, in which Paul battles with the faithful who still submit to the law of Moses, Sir Edmund suddenly exclaimed, 'Oh, how I do hate that Law.' He continued, 'I took the Law to be a person of malignant temper from whose cruel bondage, and from whose intolerable tyranny and unfairness, some excellent person was crying out to be delivered. I wished to hit Law with my fist, it being so mean and unreasonable.'

Judaism, however, believes that the Christian rejection of law as a religious discipline means the absence of a proper channel through which values are defined. One cannot speak of love without first legislating how it is expressed. Judaism is stating a truth about mankind. Mankind needs laws that are divine. The profundity of the Ten Commandments does not lie in the substance – indeed the human mind might dictate these commandments itself. Rather, the uniqueness of the Ten Commandments lies in the fact that it was God who commanded them. This means that the essence of the Ten Commandments lies in their introduction of immutable, divine law as the operating force in the universe. When God gives commandments they are universally applicable in every age and at every time. They are not subject to interpretation or modification. Thus, the commandment not to steal is as relevant today as it was in ancient Mesopotamia, and as applicable here as it would be on Jupiter or any existing or as yet undiscovered galaxy.

Moreover, there are no rewards or punishments provided in the commandments. There aren't even rationalisations of them. God does not say, 'Do not steal. After all, you would hate it if it happened to you.' There is no room for argument or rebuttal. Rather, He simply says that these ten things must be observed. Period. This is My world and these are the rules. Just do it.

When mortals make laws, they become subject to human

interpretation, and hence, manipulation. Ronald Reagan once said, 'I have wondered at times what the Ten Commandments would have looked like if Moses had run it through a state legislature.' Man has a knack for adapting laws to his own service and making them apply only to situations where it suits his fancy.

Undeniably, deep within every man and woman is the desire to do good. So why does goodness still lose out? The answer lies in the brilliance of the human mind. Infinitely clever, it can find endless justifications and rationalisations for immoral action. What do you do if you want to share some juicy gossip about someone, but know that it is wrong? Do you remain silent, or speak up? Answer: you tell yourself that this is not gossip since if you don't forewarn people about how bad a person the individual in question is, they will end up getting burned by him in business or in a relationship. In fact, we might even say that for most people, rationalising their bad behaviour is the perfect solution to the endless struggle that rages in their hearts.

The purpose of the immutable law of the commandments is to remove all this room for rationalisation of sin. Hence, the foremost aim of Judaism is to bring the world to ethical monotheism. Ethical monotheism is the doctrine that there is one God, that He is therefore the God of all people, and that God's primary demand upon people is that they live ethical and compassionate lives. One is directly dependent on the other. Without God there can be no law defining goodness. And without goodness God is a man-made idol which justifies man's selfishness.

Foremost, ethical monotheism declares that God's primary demand is that we treat our fellow human beings decently. This seems obvious. But because many religious people have adopted a belief in God without a concomitant belief in goodness, many religious atrocities have been perpetrated throughout history. The error of those who committed such evil is that while they may have been believers in God, they did not believe that God's primary demand is moral behaviour.

We have seen this error at work in Nazi Germany. What is most striking about the Nazis is that they had laws against murder. In theory the perpetrators should have been prosecuted as murderers. So, how could the Nazi state allow the murder of six million Jews to occur unpunished?

Note, in particular, that the institutionalisation of the final solution cannot have obscured the viciousness of the attack on the Jews completely. When I visited Poland, Oxford Professor Jonathan Webber, the official Jewish representative to the Polish Government's Commission on the Auschwitz death camp site, took me to see a clearing in the woods, outside the village of Tarnow. There in the sparkling green grass was a mass grave of 840 Jewish orphans whom the Nazis marched out to this pit to shoot them. But the children would not remain still long enough for the machine-gunners to put bullets through their skulls. Luckily, there were many trees, and they simply cracked their heads against the trunks.

How could these people get away with this, even at the time? Very simple. As the law was man-made rather than religious, equality did not matter. It was as helpless as those 840 children. While the Ten Commandments prohibit murdering *any* human, the Nazis assumed a right to interpret who should be classified as 'human'. Since Jews were disease-infected parasites they even deserved to be exterminated.

Judaism would claim that this type of erring could not

have happened if religion had remained an integral part of the law. Only once man was robbed of the dignity of having been created in God's image and became identified instead with pure reason, could the law develop into a political tool, to the point where aggression was not merely permissible but even imperative as *real politik.*

The Banality of Evil

It is this banality of evil that Judaism tries to combat when it says that its religious laws need to be adhered to. Witness the following statement:

> The more civilised so-called Caucasian races have beaten the Turkish hollow in the struggle for existence. Looking to the world at no very distant date, what an endless number of the lower races will have been eliminated by the higher civilised races throughout the world.

Now, compare the statement above with a rationale for euthanasia published this century:

> In nature there is no pity for the lesser creatures when they are destroyed so that the fittest may survive. Going against nature brings ruin to man ... and is a sin against the will of the eternal Creator. It is only Jewish impudence that demands that we overcome nature.

The first quotation belongs to Charles Darwin. The second one was written down by Adolf Hitler.

Note also that Darwin gave his major work on evolution, *The Origin of Species by Natural Selection*, the subtitle, *The*

Preservation of Favoured Races in the Struggle for Life. In dealing with man strictly as a biological organism in a 'great chain of being' with all other organisms, evolutionary biologists have divided the human species (*Homo sapiens*) into various 'subspecies,' or races, in the same way that other species are subdivided. *Homo erectus*, ape-like man, may have evolved into *Homo sapiens*, and someday a particular superior race among the latter may evolve into, say, *Homo supremus*, superman. It is not hard to see how the Mengeles and Eichmanns of the past, when they were injecting dye into the eyes of children, felt they were only experimenting on, what was to them, an inferior species for the benefit of a higher species, in much the same way that we experiment on chimpanzees.

You may say at this point, 'Well that is the past. But we have now learned our lesson, and we know that it is wrong. More importantly, we know how we should avoid making the same mistake.'

However, even today scientists suggest ideas that, though they seem harmless at first, have a horrendous potential. Professor Bentley Glass suggested a more objective definition of the concepts of 'good' and 'evil' whereby they would be completely divorced from their moral connotations. His 'objective' guidelines would define 'good' as what is good for the development of the species; what is not good for the development of the species; what is not good for the development of the species would, by definition be 'evil'. Glass does not make clear in each and every case what he means with 'good for the development of the species', or the list of criteria which determine exhaustively what should be excluded as simply neutral rather than bad in respect of the development of the species. Yet, others, with less precise minds, may feel free to argue that if, for example, the species includes the mentally ill, disease-carriers, those of low intellect, or physically repulsive people, the inter-breeding of whom might be considered bad for the species, then these individuals could be eliminated.

An idea which might also have such unintended potential was proposed by Nobel laureate Francis Crick, who suggested that it may be necessary to redefine the concepts of 'birth' and 'death'. He suggested that the time of birth of an infant be redefined as two days after parturition so that there would be time to examine it. Crick has also proposed redefining death as occurring when a pre-determined age were achieved. At that time the person's property would pass on to his heirs.

Modern Paganism

Though monotheism supplanted paganism long ago, paganism was never totally defeated. Having slumbered thousands of years, it has now once again reared its head, but with a twist. No longer does man worship plants and the element of fire. Rather, he now bows at the altar of human nature. The creed of this new paganism declares that anything which is natural is necessarily good. Since scientists now assume a genetic basis for almost every human aberration, the new religion labels any attempt to try and subvert one's genes as a crime against nature.

Books like Robert Wright's best-seller, *The Moral Animal*, argue that adultery is not a crime because it is natural and essential for the survival of the human species for the male of every group to seek the widest possible distribution of his gene pool. Men cannot help but stare at every woman and not to indulge is unhealthy and dangerous repression.

Since adultery is natural, it cannot be labelled sinful. Evolutionary biologists have even shown how female birds secretly sire children from mates other than their partners because of the superiority of the infiltration. And if birds can do it, why not humans? Just follow your instincts and enjoy the ride.

But, just as there is nothing inherently evil about nature, there is likewise nothing inherently good about it either. It is man who chooses to utilise nature either in conformity with, or outside, the laws of morality. It is natural for children to prefer watching television to doing their homework. It is also natural for parents to pacify their children with toys rather than give of their time. But is this good? The only real crime against human nature is not to channel our nature into actions which are life-affirming and holy. The greatest crime against human nature is to leave it in a state in which it is indistinguishable from animal nature.

Adolph Hitler remains the most written-about, perhaps the most puzzling man of the twentieth century. I maintain that this is because deep down, as with these scientists, he haunts us with his logic. Why should we not kill the mentally handicapped? Is there a rational reason for allowing a man or woman, who will always be a burden to the state and their family, to continue to live? If we have to make difficult choices between who gets treatment and care, isn't it right that we should decide against those who cannot or no longer contribute to society?

This is where the danger lies. The key in appreciating what religion may do for us is to understand that religion works because is counterintuitive. This is not to say that religion is a guarantee against atrocities. Indeed religion is demonstrably responsible for many wars and atrocities. But precisely to combat fundamentalism, the Ten Commandments were delivered by God in the form of two separate tablets, each equally indispensable to the other. The first deals with laws concerning the belief in, and absolute respect for, God. The second deals with morality and prescriptions against indecent behaviour. The message: without both the set is invalid. Without God there can be no goodness. Without goodness, the belief in God becomes a farce.

Religion is like a matchmaker who must prepare a slovenly and ill-attired young man for his first date. He has to be dressed up, only then can he make a favourable impression. Similarly, man cannot approach God with only himself on his mind. Religion begins with the premise that human nature must be modified away from narcissism and selfishness to sacrifice and honesty. Man must forgo false relationships based on manipulation and approach God with sincerity. The question, then, is how is human nature best improved?

Doing the Right Thing for the Wrong Reasons

Once a wealthy merchant came to the great Rabbi Shneur Zalman of Liadi. 'Rabbi, I had an idea to endow an orphanage that can accommodate two hundred children. But I have since abandoned the project for, after careful examination of my intentions, I had to admit I was doing it as a means of receiving respect in the community. I am doing it insincerely.'

The old master looked the merchant squarely in the eye and said sternly, 'Build it anyway! You may not mean it sincerely. But those poor children who will eat hot food and go to sleep in a warm bed, *they* will do so sincerely.'

Every action perforce embodies two dimensions. The first

is the motivation for the action. The second is the action itself. It will be noted that these two dimensions actually correspond to twin goals of personal perfection, on the one hand, and perfection of the world at large, on the other. Why we do things speaks volumes about the kind of person we are. If we give charity to get noticed then we are selfish, while if we give it because we love the poor then we are kind.

But as far as the consequences which our actions have on the world at large are concerned, our motivation is of little importance. The starving child in Sudan who eats the bread that we paid for rarely thinks about why we did it. The important thing is that he will live to see another day. Similarly, it is totally irrelevant to a bereaved parent if the drunken driver did not intend the consequences of his action. Nor will they take any solace in hearing that the drunken motorist had one too many because he was enjoying a romantic anniversary dinner with his wife.

This is the reason why Judaism insists that one must do a good deed even when one does not feel at one with it. Refraining from doing a good deed because we question the earnestness of our intention is the piety of fools. The ancient rabbis taught that man's evil inclination is a wily fox and comes to us in many guises. Sometimes, he even dons the robes of the scholar and come to us as a learned and aged sage. 'You can't help people when in your heart you know you are a hypocrite', he tells us. The key therefore is to remember that any rationalisation that obstructs us from doing a good deed emanates from the dark side of our personality. There are no exceptions.

The Art of Persuasion

How does Judaism persuade people to change? The answer to this question marks the principal parting of the ways between Christianity and Judaism. Both religions begin with the premise that man must be made better. But while Christianity argues that only inner faith and divine grace can change man, Judaism maintains that inner transformation comes about through external action.

Rather than believing that the heart fashions the hands, Judaism believes that the hands fashion the heart. We can learn to love people by first treating them decently. Correct action, as stated above, is superior to proper intention. What we do becomes an inextricable part of who we are. It is the hands which serve as the fundamental religious organ. To be a good Jew does not necessarily mean that one has the right beliefs or feelings. Indeed, Judaism has never been a dogmatic religion. Many observant Jews are agnostics, a fact which I am sure puzzles Christians no end.

Christianity, especially in its Protestant denominations, begins with the premise that man cannot achieve salvation through his own personal devices. He is entirely dependent on grace which is given freely by the Divinity. Man is too sinful, too removed from God to save himself. Unconditional faith and submission are the prerequisites for such grace being bestowed. Man must first have the right beliefs, he must embrace Jesus. Belief in Christ will then lead to righteousness of action. Reversing the order is utterly useless. Righteous action without the right motivation is hypocrisy and is the surest path to hell. The heart must first be pure.

A classic illustration of the divergent approaches adopted by both religions in the field of human action is their respective expressions for giving alms to the poor. The Christian word for helping the needy is charity, derived from the Greek word *karitos*, meaning heart. It is necessary to empathise while feeding the poor. But the same act of assisting the needy is known in Judaism as *tzedakah*. *Tzedakah* means justice. When a man knocks on your door and says that he is hungry, you must feed him, whether you feel like it or not. He may even come in an expensive suit, dampening your compassion. No matter. Feed him anyway. To do so is just and righteous, regardless whether your heart participates in the *mitzvah*. There is only righteous action. Ten to twenty per cent of your income is simply not yours, it belongs to the poor. To deny the needy man what is his due is an act of injustice, rather than a lack of compassion.

Even if you consider the needy man to be a lazy and irresponsible parasite, you still cannot withhold him his due. A bank manager who hates his clients must still produce their funds upon demand. A friend of mine who was wealthy suddenly lost everything in a bad business venture. I went around collecting for him and his family to pay their mortgage so they could continue to live in their large and beautiful house. In Judaism, charity is as much about dignity as it is about feeding one's family. If a man is subject to the humiliation of being thrown out of his own house, having lost face he will probably never again raise himself to his feet again and become self-sufficient. One wealthy man whom I approached told me that he would not contribute to the fund 'because he lives in a much larger home than me and I still see him walking around in Armani suits.' I responded that I had not asked him for his opinion of the man in need. Rather, I merely requested his support. 'Does a man need to don sackcloth and ashes to merit compassion? Judaism couldn't give twopence for one's inner denigration for the poor. Just feed them anyway. I didn't ask you to sit and cry and feel his pain. I asked you to *end* his pain.'

I often hear Jewish communal activists telling me how much better it is to have overt anti-Semitism, rather than the silent kind which only lurks in people's hearts. Rubbish! Far better to have evil in your hearts than to practise it outright. What do I care if there are closet anti-Semites? So long as they never voice or act on it.

Habit Becomes Second Nature

Maimonides explains that there are two kinds of human nature. The first is our congenital nature, our natural in-born character traits. Modern science would call this genetic pre-disposition. Some people are born passive, with a kindly disposition, others are born aggressive with a strong competitive streak. Still others are calm until provoked, and then their formidable, fiery temper shows itself. But there is also another kind of human nature, namely, an acquired one. Thus, repetitive habit can actually rewrite our genetic programming and reorient our instincts. What begins as something we do ends up as something we are.

One of Judaism's strongest beliefs is that repetitive action ultimately becomes second nature. By giving charity, once, twice, and three times, man begins to feel more and more for the victims of poverty. Take people who are born with a selfish, self-centred orientation. When they pass a beggar on the street, their natural reaction is to walk straight by and curse 'the free-loaders' under their breath. But one day, motivated by a sense of guilt or shame in the face of other onlookers, they give the beggar a few coins. The next day they do it again, and the next day again. Soon it becomes an automatic habit. Although they began as a selfish person who occasionally practised kindness, they end up as a compassionate person who cannot help but donate some coins whenever they walk by someone in need. Their practised habit has become an intuitive response. If a few days go by and they haven't found anyone to whom to give some charity, they will even feel uneasy.

The rule in Judaism is simple: by giving to charity constantly, we become charitable. Thus, it dictates that rather than a man giving, say, a thousand pounds to charity once a year, he should distribute three pounds daily for all three hundred and sixty five days of the year. It makes no difference to the poor. The same amount is given regardless! But it does make a difference to the man who gives. For when he gives regularly and repeatedly, he will change himself.

It is for this reason that Judaism thinks that organised religion – with its regular demands and routines – in particular has the capacity to change the inner soul of man. Repetition which is the norm in Jewish religious life is not an encumbrance but a programme of change.

Inner transformation is the Jewish objective. This is true of prayer, and every other religious ritual. Judaism has no desire for man to pray occasionally, but rather for man's life to become a living prayer. If man seeks to live a life in accordance with God's will, and thereby be granted the great privilege of knowing God and being in a relationship with Him, then He must do the Godly thing. Ultimately, prayer should become as integral a part of human life as having three meals a day, as intuitive as eating breakfast.

Likewise, Judaism has no desire for man to practise occasional hospitality, but rather for mankind to become hospitable. Jewish law demands that every family have guests at their weekly Sabbath table. Kindness should not be practised only when we feel kind, just as brushing our teeth should not be undertaken only when we're feeling unhygienic. Religion is not a luxury reserved for the odd moment when feeling overwhelms us. Rather, God must be built into our daily schedules so that He becomes an essential part of our lives.

Man's first obligation, after accepting God's will unquestioningly, is to make the world a better place. Humans must work to bring about a Messianic world. Any good deed must be met with unconditional applause. This is why all people must do good deeds even if it is for misguided or selfish purposes. We must never belittle people's actions by seeking to probe the depths of their hearts. This is also why the endless contemporary search to expose hypocrisy must stop.

Evil which Becomes Embedded in our Character

About two hundred years ago, a young Hassidic man travelled all the way across Russia to see the great Rabbi Levi Yitzchak of Berditchev, a sage noted for his great love of all of God's creatures. In an age in which rabbis were known for their fire-and-brimstone speeches, Rabbi Levi Yitzchak extended his love for the righteous man and sinner alike. The young man was ushered into the great rabbi's study. 'Rebbe,' he said, 'I have sinned, and I have come to you for guidance about how to atone for my sin. You see, there was a married woman after whom I lusted and she after me. To my eternal shame, we have now consummated our mutual attraction. I have come to you in guilt to expiate my sin. But before you tell me what penitence I may undertake, know that the sin was much better than it could have been. You see, before we acted on our desire, she went to the *mikveh* [the ritual bath into which a woman immerses herself seven days after her period]. So at least she was ritually clean.'

Upon hearing the man's confession, the rabbi rose from behind his desk and commanded the young man to leave his office. 'It is best that you go, for I cannot help you.' The young man was perplexed. 'I came to see you specifically. I could have been shunned by any rabbi in Russia. But you have a reputation for tolerance and loving kindness. Did I make a mistake travelling four days by train to see you?'

'I am tolerant and loving,' replied the sage, 'to most people. Because people on the whole are good. It's just that they sin and do foolish things which derail their lives, and I am here to help them on the difficult journey back to innocence. But you are different. You are not someone who sinned. You, my son, are a sinner. Had you told me that you found yourself in a room with a beautiful woman and you could not control yourself, I would have told you, *Nu, Gei veiter*, Get on with your life. Forget about it, and wash it away in a sea of good deeds. But this is not what happened. Rather, you said that she first went to the *mikveh*. In other words, this was not an act of passion. It was an act of premeditated sin. You planned your transgression. Both of you began your countdown after her period commenced. Five days till we sin, four days, three days and so forth. So I cannot instruct you as to how to purge yourself of what you have done. Your attempt to whitewash your sin has relegated you to the ranks of the incorrigible.'

The Talmud says that the first time one sins, one is seized by pangs of conscience and remorse. The second time, one becomes slightly more desensitised and indifferent to the sin. In order to deal with our guilt we continue to maintain that we are good people amidst our blatant shortcomings. We tell ourselves, 'Fine, what I have done is not the greatest thing in the world. But it's not the worst thing either.' And what happens when we commit the very same sin a third time? Why, by this time it has become for us a virtue, a *mitzvah*! We not only rationalise the sin, we now justify its commission.

So the first time we cheat on our taxes, we feel guilty. 'The State needs the money to build roads and finance social-welfare, so why am I so selfish?' The second time, we rationalise it. 'It's not so bad. It's not good either, but every-one does it. You've got to be crazy to pay all your taxes. Why should I be any different?' But by the third time, we say to ourselves, 'It's a good thing that I've withheld my full taxes. After all, just look at how the government wastes so much money on so many worthless projects. My children's univer-sity education is far more important.'

Judaism accepts that all of us make mistakes. We are not perfect people, but we must not aggravate our imperfection. If a man loses his temper with his wife, he should undertake not to repeat his callous behaviour. He should seek his wife's forgiveness and after obtaining it, he should forgive himself as well. But the moment he justifies his anger in his own mind saying, 'I'd rather not yell, but this is the only way that I get results', he has become an abominable husband. Next he might justify striking her with the same rationalisation. Between sin and being a sinner stands the human conscience. Like a virus weakening our immune system, sin will damage our character the moment we start candy-coating what we have done wrong.

Internal and External Goals

Although world redemption is mankind's first calling, the individual cannot ignore his or her own development as a good, kind, and caring human being who is sensitive to the suffering of the human family. Man must strive to make himself into a miniature Temple in which God can reside. It is for this reason that motivation, intention, and the right incentive remain highly significant in Jewish thought, albeit always of secondary importance. Even though the wrong reason will not negatively taint the good deeds we do, we have an obligation to improve first the macrocosm, the world at large, and then the microcosm, the world of man.

Hence the Jewish religion speaks of a complete *mitzvah* consisting of the Godly act coupled with the proper motivation. Our first obligation in life is toward works of public utility, to pursue love and justice and enhance the lot of our fellow man. But a significant proportion of our time must be dedicated toward ensuring that we never forget that we must also be glorious human beings, on the inside as well as the outside. Thus, for thousands of years, Judaism has insisted that even significant philanthropists, encumbered as they are with myriad business responsibilities, must still study Torah themselves. Conversely scholars of religious law and the clergy must also give charity and assist their fellow man, even though most of their time is devoted to self-refinement and piety.

To lead more holy and perfect lives, clearly, we must first embrace the redeeming quality of organised religion, with its regular routine of prayer, ritual, acts of kindness, and moral restraint. Religion is nothing without its routine. To wait and be seized by the moment is a recipe for fickle morality. This will help us to ingrain religious worship deep into our psyche where it can become an essential and inextricable part of our character. Secondly, we must do our utmost to break the cycle of pain and sin, both within ourselves, as well as in society and families.

When a woman who is barren for many years prays for a child and suddenly conceives, we call that a miracle. Poetry! Yet every day millions of women similarly conceive and we call that biology. Displaying love to one's spouse in moments of great passion or happiness is a misleading illusion. Rather, one must submit to the beauty of simple, everyday, married life. If you are experiencing marital discord, don't wait for a moment of inspiration to save your marriage and tell your spouse that you love them. Rather, embrace the routine, however initially unpleasant. Wake up every morning and give your spouse a kiss, help tidy up the bedroom, clean the dishes even if – especially if – you don't feel like it.

In mending the bridges in our lives, we should refrain from taking the short cut of acting better only in moments of great elation or triumph. Judaism conditions man to find the magic in everyday life, rather than the fireworks in the occasional and the fleeting. Religion is designed to sensitise man to the presence of God in the very fabric of nature and not only in shooting stars or a solar eclipse. Inner reorientation is a result of regular and routine patterns wherein man submits to the good because it is right and righteous, rather than because it is exciting. Life is about prose, not poetry. By discovering this in every waking moment we unearth the God who is hiding behind the veil of nature.

6

Women

Our world has changed so much over the past few generations that a man of one hundred years ago would hardly recognise anything of his world today. In no sense is this truer than in the phenomenal changes relating to the role of women in society. Confined largely to the shadows in former times, the modern woman has emerged as a man's equal in every sphere and there is hardly an area of endeavour, previously exclusive to males, that has not been thoroughly penetrated by women.

Over the last two centuries women have made significant progress in Judaism too. Just one hundred years ago women found it very difficult to study anything formally but the most basic Jewish texts. There certainly were no formal female academies of Jewish study prior to 1917 when the first Beis Yaakov women's seminary was founded by Sarah Shneerer in Cracow. With the proliferation of women's seminaries, it is today possible for a Jewish woman to engage in the same curriculum as men, mastering all the great Jewish texts. Even the Talmud, once a taboo subject of study for women, is now par for the course at many advanced women's seminaries and is taught by a rabbi in many communities.

However, there exists a general perception that religion has remained curiously lackadaisical in accommodating the needs of women, refusing to accord them equality in all religious affairs. In an age in which success outside the home is the overall delimiter of achievement, Judaism, with its praise for the more private, homebound, childrearing womanly role, would appear chauvinistic and prejudiced. In all my years serving as rabbi at Oxford, few issues have fired as many arguments as that of Judaism and gender. Students are turned off by what they perceive to be discrimination against women and many female students avoid orthodox Jewish services because they don't want to be segregated from the men during prayers.

Various other examples are cited of Judaism's discriminatory policy against women, including the prescription of different laws for men and women. Men are obliged to keep all the commandments of the Torah while women are absolved from any commandment – such as wearing a prayer shawl and reciting the three daily prayers – which are time dependent. 'Why are we hidden behind the *mechitza* [the divider in the synagogue]?' many young female students ask me, as they noisily depart our prayer services, never to return. 'Why can't I get up in front of the congregation and have an *aliyah* [call to the Torah, reserved exclusively for men in orthodox synagogues]? Why can't women be rabbis? Why must women dress modestly and remain locked behind layers of clothing?' This spills over into far more comprehensive complaints. Why the general Jewish attitude of separating the sexes? Why cannot men and women be locked together in a private room unless they are married? Why can't women dress just like men, wearing slacks, jeans, and a tank-top tee shirt? Why does the Bible specifically prohibit clothing which is not gender specific, as in Deuteronomy: 'A woman shall not wear a man's apparel, nor shall a man put on a woman's garment; for whoever does such things is abhorrent to the Lord your God'? And one could go on to complain about all the many time-dependent *mitzvahs* addressed to men.

I could try to draw upon historical Talmudic and rabbinic sources to respond individually to each of the objections raised above. Case in point, the segregation of the sexes in synagogue is based on the principle that each person approach God as an individual rather than as a family, and that any kind of distraction which might disrupt total concentration during prayers must be minimised. But the complaints are certainly correct in many ways. And one thing that has not changed and may never change in orthodox Jewish circles is a woman's more private role and her exclusion from public rabbinical duties.

Why Must the Sexes be Treated Differently?

For two reasons, I will approach the issue of gender in Judaism from the perspective of general principle. Any comprehensive and honest appraisal of those aspects of Judaism which distinguish the roles of men and women, would require the intricate analysis of complicated Jewish law far beyond the scope of this book. But, more fundamentally, the real issue at stake is not the specific differences in the roles of men and women, but the more general question, why should there ever be any differences at all? Is there really a need to dismantle all differences between the sexes?

Far from lauding the male role at the expense of women, Judaism – as stated earlier – has always maintained that the feminine transcends the masculine. The historical imperative is to move away from an aggressive approach to life – a love for war, honour and vengeance – and develop a passion for the feminine – love, compassion and a nurturing position towards our fellow man. The Messianic era will be a feminine period in which the infinite light of the God of History will shine unhindered through the currently obstructing 'male' layers of the God of Creation. It is therefore crucial, according to Judaism, that we observe the distinction between the masculine and the feminine, and realise that these are indeed different gifts from the deity.

Women must not try to duplicate the role accorded to men, because women have a more mysterious, higher function. This is not a veiled way of saying that today's women should be deterred by Judaism from pursuing every 'male' profession. On the contrary, Judaism insists that every individual maximise their fullest human potential. It does mean, however, that their religious role is less visible, more private. Men require physical signs of spirituality in order to bring out their religious devotion. For women this occurs much more intuitively. And so men may need to wear a yarmulka to help remind them that God accompanies them at all times, while women don't need an external symbol as they experience His presence more inwardly. Today there is no doubt that women are just as capable as men, and should be doctors and lawyers, presidents and prime ministers, corporate chairmen and business consultants … or full-time mothers and wives, whatever suits their fancy. But it is an essential part of the Jewish *Weltanschauung* that, even while doing a man's job, they should do it as a woman and should never abandon or compromise their inner femininity. Women can show the way to men by pursuing professional careers while still taking pride in the success of their private lives.

Modest Dress

Starting with the most practical issue, the visible difference of men and women, I argue that Judaism had the most noble intentions in insisting on the different roles of men and women. Those who have read my previous book, *Kosher Sex*, will know that Judaism is passionately convinced that it is specifically the physical pull, or 'polar attraction', between the sexes that matters rather than compatibility. Since married life and the family are the hallmarks of Jewish communal living, the Bible took extraordinary steps to ensure the maintenance of attraction between the sexes at all times and thereby the viability of long-term male-female relationships. For men and women only marry because they are magnetically and irresistibly drawn to each other. Men get excited by the nudity of limbs and bodies, because their sexual passion is largely physical. But a woman's love is much more psychological, less dependent on extraneous factors, much deeper rooted – and the same is true for their faith. For either gender, differentiation of the sexes will add spice to (and hence strengthen) relationships.

Without the strength of this attraction there would be precious little reason to cross the gender divide and relate to the opposite sex, as both men and women have far more in common with members of their own sex. What draws a man to a woman is not the fact that she is the same as him, but rather that she is his opposite. Men and women differ in far more ways than their anatomy. From the earliest age, boys play with other boys, and girls with other girls. In our teens, this begins to change and we feel drawn to the opposite sex, not because of what we have in common but precisely because of what we lack in common. Highlighting the delicate mystery which is fundamental to a woman's nature, men will only pursue women that they cannot ultimately conquer. The total submission of a woman to a man, therefore, would not only be improper, it would invite instantaneous boredom. For a man to pursue a woman in a relationship, there must always be a gap which he can never completely close; a relationship must always serve as an endless journey of discovery.

In the area of successful male-female relationships the rule is simple. If a man first does not wish to undress a woman mentally, he will not wish to undress her physically. Modest dress is a classic case in point, but any rule treating man and woman could be advanced. A wife who is normally dressed modestly elicits great passion from her husband simply by undressing. The masculine-feminine role-play invites the mind into the sexual act as an equal participant. Very few women need their husbands to dress up in lingerie for them, but men often require these artificial inducements.

Women as the more spiritual half of the human race don't need this trickery of the senses. They require a more spiritual approach. Indeed, the ancient rabbis took the more fully developed spiritual intuition of women as a lead for religious service. It accounts, they argued, for why men must wear the *tzitzis* (mini prayer shawl) which reminds them at all times of God's commandments, as well as the *tefillin* (phylacteries used during morning services), which places God's words upon the mind and heart. Women do not need external reminders as God's words are actually written on their hearts and embedded in their souls.

Masculine and Feminine Energy

We have to peel away the revealed layers of law and tradition in order to peer at the reason why Judaism's philosophy places feminine energy at a higher level than male energy. The Jewish God could not be more different from the Christian God. Jesus as deity is very much defined. He has a name, he is male, and there is a strong record of his life and actions on this earth. In Judaism, the hidden God is non-anthropomorphic (not possessed of a body) and also non-anthropopathic (transcending all emotions) because God is the source of all life, and every living creature. God is equally close to the snail as He is to the human, equally the creator of the star cluster spanning many millions of light years, as He is the source of the gnat, barely spanning millimetres. If God were more defined and had a male body, then He would be much closer to men than women, and women could justifiably speak of a religion which is misogynistic. Similarly, if God had a human as opposed to an animal form, then we could justifiably speak of a God who is closer to humanity than He is to the beasts of the field.

Certainly, the Bible uses masculine terminology in describing the deity. But far from conveying the idea that God is male, this is due to the fact that the Bible is principally a book of law, designed to curb mankind's more violent passions, so that individuals love and refrain from harming one another. In these places it is dealing with the external problems of mankind, which means that the masculine energy of creation is addressed. Similarly, a stern masculine voice is one to which men are much more responsive in matters of morality and law.

In fact, there are many instances of female imagery being

used to describe the deity, most notably the word Shekhina, depicting the divine presence which rests upon prophets and places. And the Bible distinguishes sharply between the feminine and masculine aspects of God. It uses many names for God which fall in one of the two categories. He is King, Judge, Father, Shepherd, Mentor, Healer, and Redeemer, to mention but a few of His aspects in His relationship to man. Elsewhere, in biblical and rabbinic literature, the names used to describe God include Shaddai – Almighty, Ha-Kadosh Barukh Hu – The Holy One Blessed be He, Ribono Shel Olam – Master of the Universe, Ha-Makom – The Place, Ha-Rahman – The Merciful, Shekhinah – Divine Presence, En Soph – The Infinite, Gevurah – The Mighty, Tsur Yisrael – Rock of Israel, Shomer Yisrael – Guardian of Israel, and Melekh Malkhe Hamelakhim – The Supreme King of Kings. The common denominator of all these names and descriptions is that they either convey the idea of God's awesome might (e.g. King of Kings), or they refer to God's nurturing and mothering instincts (e.g. The Merciful).

The masculine aspect of God is the immanent God of history, demonstrating peculiarly male-aggressive characteristics. This is the aspect of God which intervenes directly and at times unexpectedly in human affairs, rewarding the righteous and punishing the wicked. Like a disciplinarian father, this aspect of the Godhead reacts directly to human choice, rewarding and scolding mankind in accordance with its actions. Represented by a line (masculine), it is the God who comes down into the world to interact with human affairs, using a stick to educate man to turn from his foibles and embrace sanctified living. It is the stern God of justice. Distinguished by immanence, this side of God is involved with the small things of creation, listening to our prayers;

concerning itself in every aspect of human behaviour. This disciplinary side of the Godhead is represented mystically as a line or the harsh rod of justice.

But the feminine God of creation, represented by a circle like a woman, hovers above creation like a protecting angel, nurturing man through the endless struggle of life, always patient even in the face of human corruption and darkness, awaiting man's repentance and embracing of the light. This is the God, not of justice, but of compassion and love, prepared to forgive man and embrace him even in moments of his extreme ugliness. This is the infinite side of God, capable of giving birth to universes and endowing all creation equally with life, regardless of merit. There is no differentiation in time between past, present, and future. This is the side of God which does not get involved with the minutiae of human life or the events of history. Everything is a blur. The chairman of IBM would hardly get annoyed at a computer delivery boy whom he employs and who has driven the delivery truck recklessly. This event is far too small and insignificant to warrant his notice.

When I grew up, true to these stereotypical roles, my father was the one who always saw that my siblings and I were undisciplined and needed training. My mother was always the one who protected us and told him that we were fine and just needed room to grow. Both were right. And both parental roles are absolutely necessary. The masculine side of creation feels the need to fight demons. Therefore, the Torah gives men *mitzvahs* to do, each entailing a physical object which a man can elevate to a higher state of perfection. But there is also a feminine way of going about Godly worship, and this entails seeing, not the dragons, but the world's inherent goodness. This involves protecting the holy world from contamination. Hence, the Jewish religion has given women *mitzovs* like the observance of the Kashrut laws, which safeguard the family from eating anything which will be injurious to their spiritual makeup, and the duty of going to *mikveh*, which safeguards the holiness of a couple's sexual relations.

The Messianic Era

Rabbi Isaac Luria, a famous mystic, even wrote in the fifteenth century that the Messiah would not come until husbands starting listening to their wives, by which he meant that the Messiah would not come until men began worshipping God as women do. To an extent, the full power of feminine energy will not be realised or manifest until the male energy has finished its work. One day, the Messianic world will dawn and the world will be rid of all its ugliness. We will all live in a feminine-passive rather than the masculine-aggressive world and the peacemakers will be the real heroes and warmongers will be treated as thugs. Indeed, from a Jewish perspective world history starts with great warriors like Alexander the Great and Ceasar, changing to peacemaking heros like Gandhi and Mandela who are distinguished by their ability to forgive rather than take revenge.

Women, hailing from the infinite, are not bound by time the way that men are. Their spirituality transcends the confines of spatio-temporal existence and they are thus obligated only in those commandments which apply at all places and at all times. In the narrative of the giving of the Torah at Mount Sinai, we read, 'Then Moses went up to God; the Lord called to him from the mountain, saying "Thus you shall say to the house of Jacob, and tell the Israelites: … if you obey my voice and keep my covenant, you shall be my treasured possession out of all the peoples. Indeed, the whole earth is mine ..."' (Exo. 19:3 NRSV). The ancient rabbis explain that the meaning of 'the house of Jacob' is the women, while 'the Israelites' refers to the men. Thus, God commanded the study of the Torah and the observance of the commandments to the women before He commanded it to the men.

About six years ago, a young Jewish woman in Oxford wrote to me that it was tragic that the very potent Jewish feminine energy had not been used to spearhead a global Jewish renaissance. I told her that I agreed with her and that it would probably be our women who will lead Jewish awareness and renewal. Surely this should be the ultimate goal of the feminist revolution: to topple the walls which separate spirit from matter and soul from body, finally to bring true harmony between masculine and feminine energies. Men are the ones who perceive a duality in existence. They see the evil and rush to vanquish it. The women take a higher view and perceive the possibility of union within all existence. Our world is being increasingly ruled by fragmentation and isolation. The feminine energy is one of sharing and inclusiveness. Women today, with their higher and more immediate powers of spiritual insight, can once again teach the world the relevance of religion to contemporary living and help mankind discover the underlying spiritual energy which pervades and unites all that is. Men and women must realise their respective, equal roles and strive to complement each other in a shared struggle to improve life.

Now is the time when women can raise to true prominence the subtle power of feminine energy and, for the first time in history, overcome aggressive male spirituality. Every commandment in the Torah involves something which is *done*;

something which is *practised*. The only two feminine exceptions to this rule are *mikveh*, and Sukkah, which a Jew must enter into and live in for the seven days of the feast of Tabernacles. These two constitute the only *mitzvahs* which completely surround the individual. The man of faith is encompassed and engulfed by something holy and nourishing. The waters of the *mikveh*, resembling the cleansing waters of Eden, have the capacity to cleanse what increasingly seems a polluted planet. Immersion in the *mikveh* and safeguarding the purity of the Jewish home is, as mentioned above, an entirely female commandment.

Our rabbis explain that space is masculine in nature, whereas time is feminine. Space is about conquest, territorialism and possession. Furthermore, to enter space one must take action and physically go there. But, as mentioned earlier, time is something which overtakes one subtly even if one does not make any effort at spirituality. Our women can teach the whole world of the importance of time and relationships over space and acquisition. Throughout history we have proved we can use our strength to slay the demons around us. Perhaps now it is time to learn how to nourish the Godliness within us. Our women will spur that movement.

Today's Defeminisation of Women

Why is it that modern women are as blinded as men have traditionally been? Contemporary social commentators have long discussed the emasculation of today's men at the expense of proactive women who are taking male jobs and proving that they can not only compete with but even overshadow men in the universities and professions. There is no doubt that for thousands of years women were deprived by men of a basic right to make the most of their lives and maximise their fullest potential. This is a crime which is correctly being righted at present. But at what price today?

Rather than only speak of the emasculation of men, we should also speak of the defeminisation of women. It has become common in the modern era for a woman who has chosen mothering as her life's calling to answer with unease when a professional woman enquires as to her career. Ludicrous euphemisms like 'homemaker', or the downright ridiculous 'domestic engineer', are used to help conceal this embarrassment. Being far removed from the dominant role-model, the woman (or man) who has chosen to be a facilitator is subtly encouraged to drop her convictions. And so, women, the agents of feminine values, have less and less time for family or their marriage and are fast becoming apostles of antiquated virtues – money, power, fame.

The purpose of the Jewish social revolution is to make the entire world, especially men, more feminine. It is to teach man that success at home with family is more important than success in the marketplace. But it appears as though the undeclared purpose of the modern world is to reverse this. University students are taught that their highest calling is to give themselves to humanity; to be a great man or a great woman. Personal growth and personal fulfilment are the catchwords of today's young generation. I know many husbands and wives who have divorced their spouses because they felt that they were not 'getting enough' out of their relationship because 'you have an obligation to yourself'. The idea of parenting is hardly as romantic as it once was and is therefore put off. People have a single child, and then complain endlessly how they find it impossible to cope. Who, then, will raise tomorrow's children? I am not saying it should be the mother only. Rather, a woman must teach her husband to raise the children as well through her magical feminine example. Aggression is not a good thing in either men or women. Blind ambition is debilitating in both.

So why should women be proud of competing with men at the expense of their own precious feminine gifts? What chimera are they chasing? Although they are achieving great things in the professions, their principal source of satisfaction should come from the quality of their relationships rather than the size of their bank account. Isn't that what they want from their men, too? The mistake that men have always made, and that women are increasingly making, is that they judge themselves according to what they *do* rather than according to what they *are*. But sons, daughters, brothers, sisters, mothers and fathers, these are the things we *are*. If you stop practising medicine you are no longer a doctor, but even if you stop loving your parents you *are* still their child. My wife is respected among the students of Oxford University, more than I am. This is mostly for her character rather than her worldly 'achievements'. Many of the female students who are her friends look up to her despite the fact that, while having a professional career in accounts, she dedicates her life to mothering and is proud of it.

It will take accomplished women who are proud of and celebrate their feminine gifts to overcome the masculinisation of today's women. Look at Rose Kennedy, who died four years ago at the age of 104, and what difference she made to the world. Though she was never embraced as a role-model for American women, she became the matriarch of the legendary Kennedy clan. Many attribute this to the fact that she dropped her career to raise nine children and always remained in the background. Once, when asked in an interview why she dedicated her life to her husband and children rather than herself, she responded that had she made something of her own career, she would only have given one great person to the world. But as a mother she was able to deliver not one, but nine strong personalities who had an extraordinary impact on the world. She was like the artist who crafted treasures that were appreciated by all, rather than painting self-portraits all the time.

Bringing Redemption to the World

In counselling married couples I am sometimes accused of being biased in taking the wife's side. I agree that I have this bias. Men, particularly husbands, seem to have a defective sexual nature. They have an extremely short sexual attention span. A wife needs to teach her husband to love a personality more than a body. To love foreplay and hugging as much as sex. And to value a relationship as something other than a means to an end. I believe firmly that women have a power to bring redemption to men. Through marriage and sharing his life with a woman, a man will learn to be more feminine.

The main lesson a wife can teach her husband is to be satisfied with her love and that of his children, rather than feeling he needs the adulation of the world in order to survive. There is a feminine softness that men must somehow bring into their characters. If they don't get it from their wives, where will it come from? Who will lead self-obsessed men to God if not the women who possess a naturally higher spiritual sensitivity than men? Wives who push their husbands onto ever higher planes of achievement are doing them a profound disservice. Rather than neutralising their masculinity, they are reinforcing it.

Of course a woman can have a career. Women should do whatever brings them most personal satisfaction. They are just as smart and capable as men. One look at today's society makes that fact patently obvious. But apart from being a lawyer, doctor, or investment banker, they should still derive their primary satisfaction from the fact that they are wives and mothers, rather than professionals. Isn't this what a wife would also expect from her husband? That what pleases him most in life is not that he is chief executive of a large corporation, but that he has the love and admiration of his wife and children?

I believe deeply in work as an important and integral part of self-fulfilment and satisfaction. Nevertheless, our work should always be on the periphery of our existence, rather than central to it. Our deepest satisfaction must come from being facilitators, and enabling others to be happy. Women teach us the beauty of illuminating others rather than always insisting on being in the spotlight. We must find our truest fulfilment in being parents, brothers, sisters, friends, and contributors to our community and society. The Talmud says, 'The mother cow has a far greater desire to feed her calf, than the calf has a desire to drink its mother's milk.' Real human satisfaction is derived from giving rather than receiving, from being needed rather than from needing.

7

Suffering

When the L'Chaim Society first had the privilege of hosting Elie Wiesel to lecture to Oxford's students in 1990, he was asked by a student at my home whether or not he still believed in God after the Holocaust. He responded, 'Of course I believe in God after the Holocaust, and my belief in Him has not wavered even a bit. But because I believe in Him, I am very angry at Him. He does exist. There can be no question of that. But why then did He allow this to happen?'

The existence of suffering is the greatest challenge to faith because it undermines the most central premise of faith which states not only that God exists, but that He loves his creatures. This implies that He cares and listens, and that every time a human being aches or grieves he can entreat his Creator to take notice and expect Him to come to his aid. It is, therefore, far more damaging to the belief of the faithful, and far more damning of God, if He does indeed exist, yet remains indifferent to the torment of man. A child who has been abandoned by his father could hardly care less if the parent still lives in another country, out of reach.

Immanuel Kant pointed out that if it is arrogant to defend God, it is even more arrogant to assail Him. Yet the Jew in particular, and the religious man of reason in general, has always grappled with cosmic whys and wherefores. It is in part this grappling for authenticity which distinguishes the religious man of reason from the religious fundamentalist.

The latter, by intense uncritical devotion, is rendered an automaton, untroubled by reason. Judaism draws from Moses's challenges of God the idea that man must always seek to understand God and, particularly, apparently divine miscarriages of justice.

The reconciliation of the good God and the people who suffer is known in philosophy as theodicy. Clearly a people who have faced two thousand years of persecution will have evolved a highly developed concept of theodicy. So, how has Judaism responded to this challenge? In the many Jewish theodicies, all traditional Jewish responses have the common thread of implicating man for his suffering – either because of his sinfulness and ignorance, or because suffering is beneficial and redemptive – and exonerating God. The very fact, incidentally, that so many different theodocies appear is a testimony to the inadequacies of each.

The pregnant question is whether the implication of man is an authentic Jewish response to suffering, based on the sources in the Bible, or whether it is a later Jewish attempt to honour God at all costs, once suffering became the norm for the Jewish people in their long and at times traumatic past. I suggest that the latter is true, which is why I will now attempt to outline the Jewish response to suffering based on the early examples of the Jewish patriarchs and prophets.

Suffering and the Patriarchs

As mentioned earlier, the Torah is not a history book but a book of instruction. When it recounts the interaction and dialogues between the Almighty and the giants of Jewish history it is recounting these stories for posterity so that we may emulate their response. What we will discover is that our biblical forebears always did the opposite when confronted with suffering, namely, they exonerated man. Indeed, the approach of exonerating God at human expense is highly inadequate, even sinful. No wonder people find it highly unsatisfactory. Righteous people who suffer look at themselves and find it difficult to accept that their deeds have been so awful as to warrant unfair tragedy.

In every case where a great biblical figure was confronted with the suffering of humanity, he was quick to intercede on the suffering party's behalf. Never once did he accept divine wrath. When God came to Abraham and informed him that He would crush Sodom and Gomorrah, cities which Abraham knew deserved punishment for their phenomenal iniquity, did he point his finger towards them, bowing his head? In one of the noblest moments recorded in the Bible, Abraham pounded with his fist and demanded, 'You are the Judge of the whole earth. Shall You not practise justice?' (Gen. 18:25) That the most righteous man on the planet could defend the most wicked, and entreat God for clemency, is a remarkable phenomenon that we should all take to heart.

Similarly, in the fifth chapter of Exodus, Moses offers a complaint to God. It is significant because it serves as the very first challenge recorded in the Bible claiming a divine miscarriage of justice towards His people. Moses had been sent by the Almighty to demand the Jewish people's release from Pharaoh. What resulted from this first encounter and his demand to 'let my people go,' was that not only did Pharaoh refuse to free them, but he gave orders that the burden of the Jews was to be intensified – straw was to be withheld from their building of bricks, despite the requirement to fulfil the same building quota per day. 'And Moses returned unto the Lord and he said, "Lord, why have You dealt ill with this people? Why is it that You have sent me? For since I came to Pharaoh to speak in Your name, he has dealt ill with this people; neither have You delivered at all Your people.'"

But, for me, the most inspiring story of the entire Bible is that of Moses in the wake of the Jewish sin of the golden calf. The Bible records that after smashing the two tablets of the law into a thousand pieces, Moses again ascended Mount Sinai for forty days and forty nights in an effort to mollify God and reverse His decision to destroy the Jewish nation. Indeed the Bible uses the words *vayechal Moshe*, Moses pleaded with God to forgive the Jews to the point where he became physically ill. He was coughing up blood, but still he would not relent. When God still does not forgive the Jews, Moses offers a statement which must easily pass as the greatest expression of chutzpah, or effrontery to the Creator anywhere in the Bible. 'Now if You will forgive the people', he says, 'then good. But if You don't forgive their sin ... blot me out, I pray You, from the Torah which You have written' (Exo. 32:32). Moses chooses self-destruction rather than allow a catastrophe to happen to his people, no matter how sinful they have been. Where else in the history of apocalyptic literature does a human admonish the Master of the Universe to remove his name from a divine work so that he will not be associated with the terrible deed of having failed to save his nation and force the deity to compassion?

When I hear this passage in the Torah read every year in synagogue, I still get goosebumps. It is quite simply the most beautiful defence of human life ever recorded. Moses tells us that one must love all of God's creatures with an infinite love, and even risk divine disfavour in an effort to alleviate all human misery.

The Injustice of Suffering

Whereas Islam translates as 'submission to God', and Christianity advocates the leap of faith, the word *Yisrael*, Israelite, means 'he who wrestles with God.' The potent Jewish message is that the biblical response to suffering is to wrestle with God.

Since man is in a relationship with God, he has the right to make certain demands which are necessary for the sanity of their relationship. All of Judaism begins with the simple premise that man needs health, happiness, and financial sustenance in order to serve God. Jacob prays to God 'If God will be with me and … grant me bread to eat and clothes to wear, then it will be possible for me to make the Lord my God' (Gen.). It urges alleviation, rather than meekness, beseeching and demanding from God a cessation of the plague. Here lies the reason why through torture, inquisitions, pogroms, crusades and massacres the Jewish spirit has never broken and the Jewish flame has never been extinguished. Auschwitz fired the Jews' higher commitment to banish suffering from the earth.

In the movie *Shadowlands*, the celebrated Oxford author C.S. Lewis first embraces a position of Christian acquiescence as the proper response to suffering. The classic dualist approach maintains that suffering is necessary to discern between pain and true happiness. His dying wife tells him that the happiness which they experience together now, the fact that she is alive and they are married, is directly dependent on the impending tragedy of her death. He accepts this position so long as she is alive, but as soon as she dies, the once submissive Lewis becomes angry with the religious platitudes offered by his friend, the Doctor of Divinity at

Magdalen. He shouts and orders the minister to be silent, swinging his cudgel at the thought that God could somehow desire anyone's death, especially that of a good person who has caused no one harm.

According to Judaism, this is exactly the right response; not because Lewis was pained and was thus incapable of submission to the Will of God at that moment, but rather because his wife, like every decent human being, deserved a long and fruitful life. Happiness is the lot of mankind which was itself promised to us by the Almighty Creator. How could this cleric be so sanctimonious, so insensitive and so arrogant as to dismiss the death of someone else in the belief that it carried with it a cosmic purpose?

Suffering is an Aberration in Creation

The sin of justifying human suffering is especially heinous for a Jew because it shows a fundamental ignorance and betrayal of Jewish theology. Judaism sees death, illness, and suffering as aberrations in creation which were brought about through the sin of Adam in Eden. When God created the first man and woman, he placed them in His garden, a perfect world which, as becomes clear from the Bible, had no suffering.

'And the Lord God commanded the man saying, Of every tree of the garden you may eat; But of the tree of the knowledge of good and evil, you shall not eat from it; for on the day that you eat from it you shall surely die' (Gen. 2:16-17). The meaning of the verse seems straightforward, but is deceptive. When Adam and Eve ate from the tree of knowledge, they did not die on that day. In fact, Adam lived

on for more than nine hundred years! How to account for this discrepancy?

According to traditional Christianity, the meaning of God's warning that sin would bring immediate death was that Adam and Eve would not die a physical death, but a spiritual one. Thus, Christianity puts forward a body-soul dualism whereby people are viewed not as integrated beings, but as possessors of an eternal soul and an ephemeral body which, for all intents and purposes, is the vessel designed to accommodate the needs of the immortal soul. As it is only the soul that is eternal, it can once again be restored in heaven through an affirmation of belief in Christ.

But the Jewish interpretation is radically different. Being God's direct handiwork whom He created in His direct image, man was never meant to experience death. Like his Father in heaven, man was meant to live eternally. But severing themselves from the infinite source of life when they sinned, Adam and Eve began to decay. Adam brought destruction into the world. He might live on after the sin, but *then* he would succumb to death, just as every apple when detached from a tree succumbs to rot. God *condemned* Adam to a physical death.

The implications of this rabbinical exegesis on this crucial passage of Genesis are both mighty and profound. As there was never meant to be any place for death in our world, neither was there ever any plan for suffering or pain. The Garden of Eden, previously this earth, was perfect. Only now, in this interim period between life in Eden and life in the perfect world-to-come, are we ravaged by cancer, AIDS, car crashes, war, hatred, and genocide. But since it was not part of the original plan, this rabbinic teaching declares, suffering has no *meaning*. It was an error, an aberration, a mistake to be corrected, a crooked line that can still be made straight as no human was ever predestined to suffer, die, or ache.

Suffering Does not Ennoble the World

Since the Jew has no answer to the *problem* of suffering, he has no choice but to eradicate it from under the heavens. Judaism, therefore, profoundly rejects any belief in the ennobling qualities of suffering. It irritates me no end whenever people speak of how much they have learned from hardship and suffering, as if similar lessons could not have been acquired through a far less painful means. Indeed, I argue that those Jews who offer suffering a redemptive quality may still be practising the Jewish religion, but have ceased thinking as Jews.

The belief in the redemptive quality of suffering is a profoundly Christian belief. In Christianity the suffering servant, the crucified Christ, brings atonement for the sins of mankind through his own sacrifice and torment. It is absolutely essential to Christianity. Not only does suffering possess redemptive virtue, it is the only means by which man is saved. If Jesus had not suffered and died on the Cross, mankind would still be damned. Suffering is extolled in the New Testament where St Paul says: 'And not only that, but we also boast in our sufferings, knowing that suffering produces endurance, and endurance produces character, and character produces hope' (Rom. 5:3-4).

It is not difficult to extrapolate beyond this and discover how Christianity has traditionally dealt with personal suffering. Here suffering is said to have a purifying quality which purges man of sin. And for those whose sins are far too heinous, there is always hell. From there, it was not too much distance to travel for even complete secularists to maintain that suffering empowers man and makes him noble. Thus we maintain today that those who have gone through negative and painful experiences have gained the virtues of tenacity, perseverance, resolve, fortitude, and a knowledge of what is really important in life, making us wiser, nobler, more sympathetic, and more understanding.

In Judaism, however, suffering is not central to redemption. Any appraisal of suffering leads to the undeniable conclusion that suffering leads to a tortured spirit and a pessimistic outlook on life. Scarring our psyches and bringing about a twisted and cynical consciousness, it causes us to look for the insincerity in the hearts of our fellows and to be envious of other people's happiness. Undeniably, suffering can cause man to rethink his life and find wisdom as to its enhancement and the betterment of the lot of his fellow man. There is no good thing which comes through suffering that could not have come about through some more positive means.

Take someone who visits a dentist. He complains about the needle the dentist uses to numb the tooth before drilling. Yet it is he who has paid for the treatment in the first place! What the patient is really saying is this: 'I accept that your poking my gums with the needle is for my own good. But after all these years, has medical science, with all its technological leaps and bounds, not developed a means to numb a tooth without pain?' And the same applies here. Whatever good we as individuals, or the world in general, receive from suffering, can it not be brought about in a painless, joyful manner? Considering that God is infinitely powerful, He has many avenues by which to achieve His objectives.

A number of years ago I met former Beirut hostage Brian Keenan. What I witnessed was a man of great extremes. Certainly, he was in the greatest agony and pain and yet he maintained a warm and beautiful smile and wrote something extremely witty in his dedication to the book I bought, the account of his ordeal as a hostage. After speaking with him, I came to the realisation that his suffering had left him in terrible torment. The special qualities he possessed, his love for his fellow man, his warmth, his earthiness, and his optimistic view of life, were present prior to his ordeal. He did not gain them because he suffered, but rather his greatness lay in the fact that he retained these beautiful traits in spite of the fact that he suffered. Speak to any Holocaust survivor, even the most noble and celebrated, like Elie Wiesel and Simon Wiesenthal, and ask them what they have gathered from their suffering aside from loneliness, heartbreak, and misery and whether this outweighs the affirmation in the goodness of man which they also experienced, but which they would have experienced anyway.

Though my personal suffering is, thank God, on a much smaller scale, I believe that my parents' divorce drove me to a deeper understanding of life, and a greater embrace of religion. And yet, I know people who have led completely privileged lives and yet are extremely deep in their philosophies of life and very devoted to their Judaism, far more than myself. And I would say that they have the advantage, because I carry baggage which those who were raised in happy homes will fortunately never be saddled with. Having served as a rabbi to university students, I can attest to the fact that those who were raised in happy homes in which their parents gave them love and attention are the most healthy, balanced and loving. Those who were neglected or ignored

by their parents can also be positive and loving. But it involves a considerable effort first to undo the scarring of the past.

For two thousand years Jews have longed for the Messiah and the perfect epoch he will usher in. As a believing Jew, I too call out in my daily prayers for his imminent arrival. But I know that my motives are not what they should be. A righteous man calls out for the Messiah for the right reasons. He wants God and goodness to be a tangible reality on earth. As for me, I have a long way to go in my personal development. Like so many others, I still pray for the defeat of evil. I detest the sight of husbands and wives who divorce each other. I want the Messiah because I continue to bear pain well into my adult years. My insecurities cause me to work endlessly to distinguish myself with lectures and books, so I pray for a time when competition and envy will no longer be the motivating forces of mankind. But as far as each of us is concerned, no man or woman is deserving of pain and we must protest to God for every human tear shed.

The only response to pain is to wage an incessant war for its destruction and never dignify any of these purely evil happenings by attributing to them significance or virtue in any measure. Every time we betray our dignity by defending the ennobling qualities of suffering or by saying that certain people are sinful and deserve to suffer, we simultaneously weaken our resolve to uproot injustice from the earth. Every time we substitute a campaign for its destruction with theodicies to explain it away, we make the mistake of channelling part, and at times vast amounts, of the energy needed to combat it into an attempt to understand it.

Did the Victims of the Holocaust Deserve to Die?

The worst offenders against the Jewish principle are those who justify the suffering of their fellow man. Even the Jewish dead of the Holocaust have been condemned to their fate by 'well-intentioned' preachers of the faith, offering various explanations of Jewish sin to warrant the extermination of European Jewry. They inform us, by virtue of their own prophetic natures, no doubt, that the high rate of Jewish assimilation and inter-marriage in pre-war Germany kindled God's wrath against the Jews. 'The Holocaust was bound to occur in a generation in which Jews were more proud of being German than Jewish.' Alternatively, they tell us of how Zionism was a Godless religion which sought to supplant Godly destiny with human effort and how the Holocaust reminded the Jews that without God they were utterly vulnerable, amidst any attempt to carve out their own national homeland.

One must ask what magnitude of arrogance any individual must have in order to condemn six million victims, none of whom they ever knew or met. This is aside from the fact that any writer who advances a theory of Jewish culpability is simply ignorant of history. The vast majority of those who perished in the Holocaust were not the Jews of Germany. On the contrary, since they were well aware of Hitler's intentions from the original Nuremberg laws of 1933, many had the good sense to get out in time. No less than seventy five per cent of German Jews survived the Holocaust. It was the devout and religious Jews of Poland who in the main made up the ashes of the crematoria of Auschwitz, Belzec, Büchenwald, and Treblinka. Moreover, more than one million children died in the Holocaust. What was the misdeed that warranted their extermination? As Rabbi Irving Greenberg wrote, 'Now that [the victims of the Holocaust] have been cruelly tortured and killed, boiled into soap, their hair made into pillows and their bones into fertiliser, their unknown graves and the very fact of their death denied to them, the theologian would inflict on them the only indignity left: that is, insistence that it was done because of their sins.'

Is AIDS a Punishment for Promiscuity?

Similarly, I would contend that it is specifically the doctor who sits late at night in search of a cure for AIDS who has done more to advance the Jewish response to suffering than the rabbi who tells us either to submit to the inevitability of terminal illness, or even worse, that AIDS is a divine punishment for sexual immorality and promiscuity. I once sat at a public lecture in Australia delivered by a renowned rabbi. The lecture took place in the mid 1980s when the world was trying to come to terms with the ravaging spread of the AIDS epidemic. When asked by one of the listeners if the rabbi felt AIDS to be a divine curse against a sexually promiscuous generation, he stunned the audience with his response: 'Who says it has to be a curse? In my opinion, it is a blessing.' He meant of course that AIDS would curb extramarital and gay sex. While some of the members of the audience applauded, a whole stream of people immediately walked out, thoroughly alienated.

His words contradict everything that Judaism stands for in the form of a good, loving, long-suffering God who asks His creatures to emulate His mercy and compassion. When something like AIDS begins to kill human life, our job is to kill the disease and save people. By making his statement, this rabbi, however illustrious, brought shame to his profession. I can personally attest to the fact that some of Oxford's leading researchers who are at the forefront in finding a cure for AIDS might be doing so more out of a desire to win a Nobel prize than to serve the cause of humanity. Yet even these scientists are more in tune with the biblical response to suffering than many observant Jews.

Suffering is Irrational

This style of theodicy leaves me frustrated and angry. This is not what God wants us to do. He does not expect us to take a remote, analytical perspective when examining tragedy. I don't care for the reasons you can come up with. I don't care to know what God had in mind when he allowed the Nazis to murder millions. Or why we are now struck by a new plague. Suffering is not a thought that can be combated with argument. Reason and deductive logic are useless weapons in this battle, as powerless as the minds of Talmudic geniuses in the face of brutal bayonets. Rabbis who try to give meaning to explain away disaster as punishment for Jewish sin are an embarrassment and should be censured.

Unfortunately, all too often those who do tend to justify suffering are members of the clergy such as the Australian rabbi. In their own misguided way they believe that they are doing God a service. Under the impression that his main responsibility to his community in the face of tragedy or pain is to provide comfort by offering cosmic whys and wherefores, the average rabbi or priest will say: 'We cannot understand the ways of God, but we must still believe that everything which God does is for our best. His ways are not our ways, etc ...' Is religion really that blunt?

The Jew is a creature of history who always raises his head to hope against hope. A true minister of religion teaches his flock to be defiant when unconquerable illness overtakes a parishioner. Never bow your head in subjugation and never capitulate. Always fight for life, always beg for mercy, never condemn your fellow man. Note that Moses's complaint to the Almighty 'Why have you let so much evil come upon this people? Why is it that you have sent me?', clearly demonstrates how he responded to the suffering of the Jewish people. He did not ask God to explain what good the Jews received from their enslavement. Nor did he request that God explain to him the cosmic justification for the enslavement of the Jews. Rather, he simply demanded, in the strongest possible terms, that the Almighty bring the harrowing enslavement of the Jews to a close.

As I stated above, there is no answer to the problem of suffering. Positing an answer means being reconciled to a problem. But there is a response. We must use our pain not to look for reasons, but to demand the Messianic era. We must turn our pain to something life-affirming and good. We must not question why innocent Israeli soldiers die in battle at the age of eighteen in defence of their homeland in the face of incessant war. Rather, we must arm ourselves for the affirmation of life and defend ourselves, but at the same time search for peace. We do not seek to understand 'why' it happens, but to prevent it from ever happening again.

Theodore Herzl, the father of modern-day secular Zionism, approached the Kaiser of the German Empire in a private audience at the turn of the century, with his idea of building a Jewish national homeland in Palestine. The Kaiser laughed and said, 'In order for that to happen, you would need three world empires to fall.' One by one, they all fell (the Ottoman Empire, which controlled Palestine prior to World War I; the German Empire, guaranteeing Palestine for the Lutheran Church; and Czarist Russia, guaranteeing Jerusalem for the Eastern Orthodox Church). Seventeen years later all of those empires had disintegrated. If even secular Jews like Herzl never gave up hope, how dare a rabbi teach his congregation to do so!

Sparring with God

I watched the film I mentioned above, *Shadowlands*, with two close friends, one of whom is Mormon, the other Christian, both devout in their religious observance. As we drove home from the film my Mormon friend felt C.S. Lewis's response to be blasphemous. 'God has a reason as to why we suffer. It is always and must always be to our benefit, since God loves us. Human beings just have to understand their limitations.' My Christian friend was slightly less submissive. His response was that, of course, in the movie it appeared as though the woman was completely innocent and that she didn't deserve this horrible and tragic end. But who were we to know whether or not she deserved to suffer? While suffering is not good, God is always just and everything which man gets, he deserves, both the good and the bad.

'What are you guys talking about?' I asked them. 'Do you really think that God needs you to defend Him? Are you so arrogant as to believe that you know for sure that this woman was guilty, and deserved to suffer? What of your obligations, incumbent upon you from God Himself, to affirm life? If this woman was suffering and you were a doctor, you would be under a religious obligation to save her. Why not take up her defence in the face of the Almighty as well?' God does not need our defence; human beings do. God is not vulnerable. He does not suffer the way that humans can. He is eternal. But humans are defenceless, they ache, and they die. They crave our support and our love.

Judaism recognises the existence, even the need, for dual roles which sometimes contradict. For example, when a child misbehaves, his parent is obviously cross and warns him to behave. Yet, even while reprimanding the child, the parent fully understands that it is natural, even desirable, for a child to run amok as children do. In fact, if the child sat still throughout the day, or if at five he showed the quiet and mature restraint of a thirty-year-old, his parent would drag him to a psychiatrist. So, the role of a child is to misbehave, and the job of the parent is to correct the child and maintain discipline. Each party carries out his role legitimately, although they are in conflict.

Human beings are charged with the eternal pursuit of love and justice, even if it means sparring with the Creator. 'The secret things belong to the Lord our God, but the things revealed belong to us and to our children forever, that we may follow all the words of this law' (Deut. 29:29). The real question which should be posed to God upon witnessing a child with leukaemia, or a collective Holocaust, is not, 'Please God, explain to us why this happens and how it fits into Your overall plan for creation', but rather, 'Master of the Universe, how could You allow this to happen? Was it not You who taught us in Your magnificent Torah that life is sacred and must be preserved at all costs? Where is that life now? Was is not You who promised that the good deserve goodness and not pain? Where is Your promise now? By everything which is sacred to You, I demand that this cease, and that the person recover immediately.'

Far from being an affront to divine authority, these words are part of the human mandate. Remaining passive in the face of human suffering is a sin against both man and the Creator. When a Jew protests to God, therefore, it is not a challenge to divine providence because we are not challenging His authority or asserting that He has not noticed the problem. Neither are we thereby maintaining that nothing positive can result from suffering or that God's plans have gone askew. Rather what we are saying is this: 'We believe that You are a good and Just Creator. But You are also all-powerful and would it not therefore be possible for You to bring about this desired end in a less painful means?' We are asking God to change the means He employs to achieve His always just ends. As for the many who argue that indeed suffering ennobles the spirit, would they then pray to the Almighty that He visit even greater suffering on mankind to induce further ethical merit? Would they also subject their children to suffering in order to build their character?

Battling with God over human suffering is not mere emulation of the patriarchs. They were taught this mighty lesson by God Himself. The ancient rabbis point out that God prodded Moses to defend the Jews when He sought to destroy them over the golden calf. The biblical verse reads 'And now [Moses] leave me so that I can devour [the Jewish people] immediately' (Exo. 32:10). Moses had not even begun to speak, before the Almighty commanded him not to interfere! What God was indicating to the great lawgiver was this: Moses, I have just told you that I plan to annihilate the Israelite nation. How can you just sit there and listen to that?

What are you going to do about it? Are you just going to sit there? By telling him not to interfere before he had even uttered a peep, the Almighty was telling him that although divine justice demanded their death, none of this was his business. Instead, as a human being, he was obliged to discharge his obligation of defending humanity at every turn. As in the example of the parent and child, the God-man relationship involves contradictory threads. God's occupation is to steer the world in the manner that He sees fit. But our role as humans is never to reckon with God's reasoning, but rather to promote those values which He conveyed as being supreme, namely life, compassion, goodness, and hope.

It is here where we can appreciate the centrality of Messianism to Judaism. Messianism represents a stubborn Jewish refusal to accept the world the way it is, and the demand it return to its original state of perfection. 'Such is life' is not a Jewish statement. The Jews are the progenitors of so many of the worlds 'isms' – such as secular humanism and communism – because the search for utopia does bear a Jewish copyright. They constantly seek either to return to the promised land, and when that is not possible, to build a new promised land themselves. Thrice a day, the Jews recite, as part of the very last prayer of each of the prayer services, the ancient dream of 'perfecting the world under the sovereignty of God.'

Conquering Death

Man is a dreamer, and his dreams result from an inexplicable inner conviction that he is indeed capable of making the impossible probable. When President John F. Kennedy spoke in 1961 of landing a man on the moon before the end of the decade, he was laughed at in an age when even commercial airline flights were still in their infancy. But a team of dedicated scientists and researchers set forth to translate that dream into reality. For the Jew, the same desire to translate all dreams into reality even includes the dream of triumphing over death. Not only has the Jew never made peace with suffering, he has made no pact with death either, refusing it any latitude. Rather, he cries out to God to keep his promise that 'death shall be defeated.'

In the true story upon which the movie *Lorenzo's Oil* is based, the Catholic parents of a child who is ill with a terminal brain disorder are told by doctors and professors that their child will unquestionably die within twenty-four months. Their priests urge them to accept the boy's fate and to offer him up to Jesus. But the parents reject both pronouncements and embark upon a two-year search for a cure to their son's illness. Although neither have any medical training whatsoever, they go to libraries and educate themselves in the body's immune system in order to find a cure. They refuse to surrender to death, and the spectacular fruit of their effort is 'Lorenzo's Oil', the cure which has saved the lives of tens of thousands of children suffering from ALD throughout the world.

This is the only authentic Jewish response to the problem of suffering: to join with God as junior partners in creation and to correct the world's ills and right its wrongs. As a creature made in the image of God, we should never, never succumb to fate in silent acquiescence. We must act like the human body's immune system. Whenever it witnesses even the tiniest germ, it immediately declares war on the alien presence which threatens the overall health of the body. It is not the purpose of the body's immune system to understand why the body suffers and why it has been affected by illness. The same applies to the human view of suffering. When someone is in pain, when there is a Holocaust, we don't need fifty rabbis and priests springing into action, pulling out their word processors, and writing books explaining how God is good despite what we are witnessing. We need millions of people springing into action saving lives and alleviating anguish. And we must cry out to our Creator and demand that He bring an end to this suffering and give what we all deserve: prosperous, joyous, and happy lives.

The Town Beyond the Wall

One of the most powerful modern pieces of literature on the subject of suffering is Elie Wiesel's *The Town Beyond the Wall*. This challenge to the Divine is perhaps best contained in the character of Varady, a former scholar who has become a recluse, who emerges to preach a sermon to the town:

> He emphasised the strength of man, who could bring the Messiah to obedience. He claimed that liberation from Time would be accomplished at the signal of man, and not of his Creator ... 'each of you, the men and women who hear me, have God in his power, for each of you is capable of achieving a thing of which God is incapable! ... [man] will conquer heaven, earth, sickness, and death if he will only raze the walls that imprison the Will! And I who speak to you announce my decision to deny death, to repel it, to ridicule it! He who stands before you will never die!

Conventionally, we think of God and Man as being vastly

unequal in their dialogue, God being omnipotent and the human protester merely His creature, a pawn to be moved at will. But in Wiesel's *The Town Beyond the Wall*, we find a significant inversion of this relationship. Norman Lamm, describes it as 'a keen awareness not only of man's power but also of his self-consciousness as an autonomous agent. It is not rational or even mystical explanations that Wiesel is seeking but rather human approaches and, even more, a confrontation with the God who permits suffering' (*Faith and Doubt*, 1971).

This dynamism in our relationship with God because of the existence of suffering also extends to our relationships with others. One of Wiesel's main characters, Pedro, says, 'The dialogue – or ... duel ... between man and his God doesn't end in nothingness. Man may not have the last word, but he has the last cry. That moment marks the birth of art ... and friendship is an art.' In other words, the meaning of suffering is discovered when we protest against it to God, and the most effective way of dealing with suffering is to extend ourselves to other humans in friendship, which is an art in the same way that Wiesel's book is art. Later in the book Wiesel writes, 'Camus wrote somewhere that to protest against a universe of unhappiness, you had to create happiness. That's an arrow pointing the way; it leads to another human being. And not via absurdity.'

In this respect I maintain that it was specifically the less orthodox, and in many cases completely non-observant Jews – the pioneering Zionists who built the State of Israel – who had the only correct response to the Holocaust. While the more traditional Jews grappled with theodicy the Zionists set themselves to work even harder toward the creation of a Jewish state. The response to death is life. The response to the destruction of the Jewish nation in Europe is the rebuilding of the Jewish homeland in Israel. They understood intuitively that the true Jewish response to suffering was not to attempt to understand it, but rather to wage war against it. I applaud their efforts. Many religious Jews owe many secular Jews a tremendous debt of gratitude for the brave way soldiers have defended and continue to defend the Israeli nation. But similarly, secular Jews owe religious Jews a debt of gratitude for keeping alive the dream that the Jews would once again become a nation settled in their homeland. And this in itself should spur religious effort to create peace between the two bitterly divided factions.

The Unity of Man

My wife and I are blessed with six young children. One of the worst things to witness is where the children do not display unity but rather selfishness and factionalism against their siblings. Once, on holiday with my family, we took the children for ice cream. My second oldest daughter pulled her sister's hair, and I told her that I would not be taking her inside the store unless she apologised. True to her stubborn nature, she refused. 'Good,' I told her, 'then you'll stay in the car', whereupon her older sister, the innocent victim, suddenly began to cry that her younger sister didn't mean it and that she would not go to the ice cream store without her. This was one of my proudest moments as a father.

More than anything else, God wants all his children to be close and to look out for each other. By defending man, even at the expense of the Creator, we show God that we have learned something from our constant exposure to His wondrous teachings. When people see the love and bonds forged between two siblings, it reflects gloriously on their parents. Likewise, peace on earth is the greatest manifestation of divine unity. Those who condemn their fellow man and explain how he deserves his pain, far from doing any justice to the reputation and standing of their Creator, actually do Him an injustice by fragmenting the human race.

If one could somehow encapsulate the vast contribution made to Jewish life and thought by the Baal Shem Tov and Hassidism over the past three hundred years, it would be that Hassidus taught man that in his effort to achieve proximity with God, he must learn to put his fellow man first, at times even before God, and certainly in those areas where God does not require man's protection. Indeed, the laws which regulate man's treatment of his fellow man account for a colossal portion of the Jewish Torah and living. The great sage Hillel, when asked to encapsulate the entire Torah, told a potential convert, 'That which you hate, never do unto others. This is the entire Torah, the rest being but commentary on this one principle. Now, go and study' (Shab. 30a).

Maimonides too, in his celebrated Epistle on Martyrdom, sharply rebukes a contemporary rabbi's condemnation of Jews who were living in Spain during the terrible Islamic Almohad persecutions, many of whom pondered conversion to Islam rather than face death by the sword. He shows how Moses, Elijah, Isaiah, and even the ministering angels of heaven were severely chastised by the Almighty when they came to Him with reports against His nation, even if all the evidence supported their claims. So great was God's anger, for example, at Isaiah for saying 'I sit here in the midst of a nation who have defiled and profaned their lips [with prayers to idols]' (Isa. 1:6-7), that God sent a seraph of heaven with a pan of coals to seal the mouth of the prophet.

If there is one thing that we humans must learn in the face of suffering, it is that we must approach and deal with one another with uncompromising love, a love that is not predicated on any self-interest. Until such time as we, together with our Creator, abolish every form of pain from the earth, we must bond together and comfort each other. Never can we watch someone else's pain, even that of an animal, in silence, and never dare we rationalise and explain away their pain.

To hasten the promised land of the future, man must today declare war on the world's imperfections by drowning them in endless acts of loving kindness. We will wrestle with the heavens and draw our swords against the angel of death. And notwithstanding how many unfortunate casualties we take in the interim, in the words of Winston Churchill, 'we shall never surrender.' By using practical tools such as studying medicine, giving charity, and offering aid to people in need and by using spiritual tools such as faith and prayer, we live up to our highest calling of having been created in the divine image. The fault-ridden irreligious businessman who may have never stepped into a synagogue but makes a loan to a colleague in need to save him from bankruptcy is deeply in tune with his Judaism. We must employ every means – research, charity and philanthropy, comforting words and an infinite number of prayers – until such time as God recognises our deep disenchantment with the world and steps in to rid the world of those ills which lie outside human reach.

The Holocaust

We have reviewed Judaism and attempted to portray it as a modern, living faith. But where do we go from here? What indeed is the best way forward for the Jewish nation to ensure its survival and future blossoming? In fact, in an age which prides itself on its rationalist bent and technological orientation, how can any religion long survive? These questions are especially pertinent to Judaism. The Jewish people continue to be no more than a blip on the map. Less than three out of every thousand people in the world are Jewish, and out of that number only about half are in some way observant. We have survived this long, but increasingly young Jews find little reason to identify and affiliate.

Certainly, there are some points of light. More Jewish day schools than ever before are opening around the globe, and kosher restaurants and Jewish bookstores now dot the Western landscape. In the State of Israel a phenomenal religious revival is taking place which has created a mass movement of hundreds of thousands who are returning to the faith.

Yet these beacons seem continually overcast by the overwhelming shadow of darkness caused by the abandonment of Judaism by millions of Jews the world over. Even today, there is barely a Jew who would agree to be buried outside a Jewish cemetery. But the main Jewish organisational body in Britain, the United Synagogue, only continues to survive with a high membership of approximately sixty per cent of

British Jews because joining is the only way to guarantee a plot in a Jewish cemetery. It seems that dying as a Jew has much more meaning for our people than living as one.

How can this exodus from Judaism be reversed? Can the Jewish people surmount the trial of acceptance and success in the same way that they have always overcome the trial by fire and suffering? Or are we destined to witness slow and gradual demise on many fronts?

Unhealthy Obsession with the Holocaust

An outsider who studies modern Jewry and its educational institutions would be forgiven if he concluded that before the Holocaust nothing of significance ever took place in Jewish history. In the area of Jewish fundraising, raising money to build a Holocaust museum or memorial is always given precedence over building more Jewish day schools or other educational establishments. And in the most ironic twist of fate imaginable, Hitler rather than Moses has become the main inspiration behind modern Jewish identity. Most Jews know more about him than about Judaism's own historical leaders.

It is almost as if Jews, through stubbornness alone and a desire to prove Hitler wrong, have decided that indeed they will not die out. Jewish teenagers are no longer reared on stories of the compassion of Abraham, the hardships of Jacob, the faith of Joseph, or the prayers of Hannah to have a son. Rather, they mostly hear stories of Jews who prayed to God just before sacrificing their lives on behalf of their God and being turned into a pile of ashes. No doubt, the story of the Holocaust is a most tragic and inspiring tale of six million innocent victims who died for no other reason than that they were Jews. Anne Frank was a remarkable young woman who learned to live with hope while the whole world around her was collapsing. It is to her credit that she did not allow her heart to be scorched. But to make her diary into a modern-day Bible is a mistake. It is a sad comment on Jewish affairs that young Jews in Jewish day schools around the world have memorised her diary, but cannot even recite the quintessential prayer of Jewish faith – the Shema – in Hebrew.

Young Jews must learn that their great heroes were those who responded to the call of God and changed the earth rather than only those who were victims of the brutality of other nations. The principal Jewish places of pilgrimage must continue to be the holy land of Israel rather than the death camps of Poland, Germany, and Austria. Jews must pray at the last remnants of the Temple Mount, the Western Wall, where David sang his sweet tunes to the Lord and where Solomon exercised wise counsel in judging the nation. Where Yochanan ben Zakkai confronted the Roman emperor Vespasian to allow a city dedicated to Torah to survive his onslaught against Jerusalem. And where a broken group of survivors who had just endured the Holocaust somehow mustered the courage to fend off eight Arab nations and set up an independent Jewish state for the first time in two thousand years.

This is not to say that the Holocaust should not be taught, God forbid. Of course, it must be. And we must make every effort to immortalise the sacred memory of our six million martyrs. But Jewish education and religion must always remain the priority. The Jews have always been the nation of life and the Jewish religion has always been the faith of the living. In contrast to Christianity, with its icons of a martyred God dripping with blood adorning all the world's churches, the Jews always focused on the present. Even in the greatest trouble, the Jews still pulled out the best bottle of wine they could muster every Friday night and festival eve and toasted to life, L'Chaim. Today, however, the fixation with the Holocaust is making Judaism into a religion like Christianity, totally focused on death and absorbed in tragedy and the redemption brought about by suffering. The obsession with the Holocaust is transforming Judaism from a religion of the synagogue into a religion of the cemetery.

The Holocaust must be seen as an incredibly significant event in Jewish history, rather than its defining moment. The Jews did not become a nation in Auschwitz, but at Sinai. Their defining moment was rising to the challenge of living according to the highest moral code, not succumbing to the world's greatest brutes. We cannot have young Jews embracing their heritage out of pity rather than out of pride and joy. The place that the Nazi German barbarians selected as the main area to incinerate God's chosen people must never supplant the place where God chose to dwell among the Jews – Jerusalem – as our most important place of refuge.

Identifying through Fear

But look how Jewish thinking has responded to this challenge. For half a century now, the Jewish people have largely identified themselves through negative compulsion. Since the Second World War, rabbis and Jewish lay leaders have largely felt that their principal role is to act as scare-mongers inducing a state of commitment among the world's Jews by painting a picture of their imminent demise. They warned either about physical extermination through anti-Semitism, or spiritual extinction through assimilation. In doing so, they have inculcated a Jewish identity which revolves mostly around the Holocaust. They have held a gun to the Jewish head, telling them in so many words that if they assimilate, then all martyrs of the years 1939-1945 died for nothing.

Eminent Jewish thinkers such as Emil Fackenheim have even argued that in the wake of the Holocaust a 614th commandment has come into being, namely, that we must ensure that we never lose another Jew, as this would amount to granting Hitler a posthumous victory. Others have taken this concept of negative impulsion further and argued that without anti-Semitism there would be no Jewish people.

This is not the first time. An earlier offering of this argument may be found in the writings of the seventeenth-century philosopher, Baruch de Spinoza: 'As to [the Jewish people's] continuance so long after dispersion and the loss of empire there is nothing marvellous in it, for they so separated themselves from every other nation as to draw down upon themselves universal hate, not only by their outward rites, rites conflicting with those of other nations, but also by the sign of circumcision which they most scrupulously observe' (*Theologico-Political Treatise*, 3:55).

Many modern thinkers have elaborated on this theory, the most famous being the French existentialist Jean-Paul Sartre in his book, *Anti-Semite and Jew*. He writes, 'The Jew is one whom other men consider a Jew … It is the anti-Semite who makes the Jew … It is neither their past, their religion, nor their soil, that united the sons of Israel … The sole tie that binds them is the hostility and disdain of the societies which surround them.' Rather than displaying any compassion for the Jewish people, which is what one would hope he in-tended, Sartre's words are more reminiscent of the words of the notorious anti-Semite, Carl Lueger, the mayor of Vienna, who said, 'Who is a Jew? That is for me to decide.'

Unfortunately, statistics would seem to confirm that Sartre was partially right. Whenever Jews have been accepted by their non-Jewish neighbours, they have been quick to assimilate. Now that the ghetto walls have been torn down, and Jews live and are accepted amongst the Gentile nations, their rate of intermarriage has rocketed to above fifty per cent in most Western countries. In countries where Jews are still persecuted or eyed with suspicion – like the former Soviet Union – the percentage is much smaller.

Muselmen

It will not come as a surprise that this author is absolutely opposed to using anything that reeks of anti-Semitism as the cause célèbre of being Jewish. I do not believe that the necessity of perpetuating the legacy of the Holocaust, or combating anti-Semitism, will ever effectively serve as the chief means by which Jews can consolidate or grow as a community.

The principal reason why this is wrong simply is this. Fear always has a shelf life. It is the worst possible way to sustain long-term commitment. Where is the Soviet Union today? Their vast secret police apparatus, and the terror it induced among their citizenry, was insufficient to sustain the commitment of the people. History has demonstrated in every circumstance that people grow immune to fear and become incapable of action. It can last a generation or two, but then people decide that enough is enough. Their attitude becomes, 'Go ahead and kill me already. I'm tired of being afraid.'

In stark contrast, capitalist countries like the United States who rewarded their citizens with good lives for their efforts rather than scaring them to death, have flourished. People never tire of love and pride. What is needed is the realisation that only positive reinforcement has the capacity to rebuild the Jewish nation and attract the young. Only a programme of educating the world's Jews as to the nobility of their heritage will have the capacity to reawaken a sleeping nation.

A Judaism of the living dead is, therefore, something which we Jews must strive to avoid at all costs. We cannot raise a generation of Jews who, although identifying with their Judaism, do so with no life. We must not create a generation of Jews whom we frighten into obedience and who go about their Jewish obligations as if by programming and rote. Even if the synagogues are full to the brink and day schools bursting at the seams, we will have failed if there is no passion. This constitutes the most important lesson that our history teaches us. The Jews who witnessed the revelation of the living God of history at Sinai must once again embrace their tree of life – the Torah – in order to ensure that they and their children continue to be written in the book of Jewish life.

Primo Levi was one of the Holocaust's most famous survivors – although one hesitates to call him a survivor since his suicide many years after Auschwitz resulted directly from his horrific experiences there. He wrote that the only truly original contribution of the Third Reich to civilisation was the Muselmann, camp slang for a prisoner near death – the skin-and-bone walking corpse, or living dead. The vast 'anonymous mass, continuously renewed and always identical, of non-men who march and labour in silence, the divine spark dead within them, already too empty really to suffer. One hesitates to call their death, death.' Today we risk creating an entire generation of Jewish *religious* Muselmen, young Jews who keep their religion out of a sense of guilt, fear and habit. But never from individual choice. The crematoria were capable of horrific destruction of millions of Jewish bodies, but we should never allow this fact to extinguish the light of even a single Jewish soul.

Jewish Culture

In pursuing a positive means by which Jews can today identify with their traditions, the question arises which elements of Jewish identity should be emphasised in order to resuscitate our people? Should it be the Jewish religion, or Jewish culture?

Over the past few years, books have been emerging advocating that Jewish culture is the only road forward toward reversing Jewish assimilation and that this should supplant the Jewish religion as the principal means by which Jews identify with their heritage. Alan Dershowitz's *The Vanishing American Jew* is the latest noteworthy offering in this vein. The argument basically goes like this: Ever since their emancipation, Jews have been fighting a rearguard action to prevent abandonment of religious ritual and especially intermarriage. With intermarriage at an all-time high of above fifty per cent, and still rising, we must now concede that the battle is lost. Let's throw in the towel and admit that Jewish religious identity is beyond salvation. But since even Jews who marry out and have non-Jewish children are still interested in Jewish culture, this should be promoted over religious ritual, which modern Jews find stultifying. Jewish ritual is archaic and boring and long since passed its sell-by date. Traditions like kosher food have lost their relevance to everyday life. So, let's stop attempting to bring rituals like *tefillin* back to life, and instead have our children read about Anne Frank and talk about the Spanish Inquisition. We can still all congregate together on Friday nights and retell the stories of Shalom Aleichem, even if it is not in celebration of the Sabbath. Let's transform what were previously religious observances – like the Passover Seder – into cultural celebrations.

This is a very persuasive line of thought. There is only one flaw with it, and that is that Jewish culture stinks. If culture is the main reason that we remain Jewish, then I advocate the complete abandonment of Jewish identity in favour of non-Jewish culture, which is far superior.

First, there is the simple fact that there is no unifying Jewish culture, a fact which makes a mockery of those who advocate that culture constitutes the reason why we should all draw together. My father was born in Iran and grew up with a centuries-old Sephardic-Persian Jewish culture. *Smaltz* herring and Yiddish theatre are as foreign to him as the Persian dish *Gormei subzi* is to most European Jews. Persian Jews also love eating a special stew made of cartilage of cow ankles. Anyone interested? Though my father has lived in the United States among Ashkenazi Jews for thirty years now, he has still to imbibe, or indeed enjoy, any unique Ashkenazi-Jewish culture. He still chokes on *gefilte* fish and spends a full week trying to digest *cholent* (but then, doesn't everybody?). At Persian Jewish celebrations, he sits with his Persian Jewish friends and sings Persian Jewish songs which are utterly unintelligible to his American Jewish friends, who show scant interest in them anyway.

The same would be true for Moroccan and Chinese Jews. Each has a different Jewish culture and would be utterly uninterested in that of another Jew. The story goes that when hordes of European Jews arrived in Shanghai during the Second World War, escaping the Nazis, they were approached by the local Jewish community who expressed incredulity at their claims to be Jewish. 'How could you be Jewish,' asked their oriental Jewish counterparts, 'when none of you even look Jewish?'

But even if we are to leave aside this crucial point for now and identify Ashkenazi culture as the way forward for Western European, North and South American, New Zealand and Australian Jews, still, this is doomed to failure. For overwhelmingly, Jews have voted with their feet – against Jewish food, music, and culture. Young Jews have contempt for their own culture which they have supplanted with the Pax Americana which the rest of the world is imbibing. Go to any large 'Jewish' city these days and try and find a 'Jewish' restaurant. Embark on a journey in search of pastrami and roast beef sandwiches and good old *luckshen* soup. Chances are you will first bump into ten restaurants serving kosher wantan soup and sushi. I could name five kosher Italian restaurants in New York City alone, but only one 'Jewish' kosher restaurant where one can obtain chosen favourites like warm borscht and garlic salted liver. Kosher restaurants serving proper 'Jewish' food have almost ceased to exist because the fatty foods have killed most of the clientele with coronary disease.

Let's face it. Aside from an occasional bagel with cream cheese and chicken soup on Friday night, Jews have overwhelmingly rejected classic Jewish food. And I say, goodbye and good riddance. European Jewish food is fatty, unimaginative, and lacks spice and inspiration. *Gribbenes*, a favourite Jewish delicacy made from fried pieces of chicken skin, just doesn't light my fire. The only use for boiled *flanken*, warm borsht, and boiled Jewish meats is, as far as I'm concerned, as a means to stay fit while running away from it. I am not wildly fond of *kiddush* wine either. Around my home, we only use Jewish wines either as syrup on pancakes, or as an adhesive. Have you ever watched as someone ate the jelly-like yellow substance that comes with *gefilte* fish? Did that make you proud to be Jewish?

The greatest proof of this comes from the State of Israel itself, where Arabic foods like falafel and shwarma have become the de facto food of all Israelis, Ashkenazi and Sephardic alike. The same is true of Jewish music. These days the only place where one can hear a Klezmer band is in the odd Jewish music festival which plays to fringe groups. Overwhelmingly, Jews flock to the wonderful music of Bach, Beethoven, Strauss, and Mozart. I break out in hives when I am invited to Jewish film festivals. Invariably, every offering is the same. Every Jewish film either focuses on the tortured identity of the modern Jew – à la Chaim Potok's *The Chosen* – or deals with the tortured relationship of a young Jewish girl with her overbearing Jewish mother. In either case, the film itself is always torture, and I would much rather read bad news on the internet. Jewish art and film festivals are typically held in someone's garage, while millions flock to see *Titanic* and *Saving Private Ryan*.

Goodbye to Jewish Culture

I do not claim to speak on behalf of my fellow Jews. No doubt I have deeply offended the many thousands who are far more attached to their boiled *tzimmes* than they are to the sound of the shofar on the Jewish New Year or the bright lights of the menorah on Chanukah. But my point is a different one.

Who cares that objectively speaking Jewish music, food, and culture do not match those of the Gentile West? Who cares that Jewish music or artistry never even came close to matching those of the Christian Renaissance artists? The Jews were never meant to be famous for their culture or for their painting. Jewish history just isn't as glaringly exciting as French or English history with their 'great' stories of battles and victories, and ye olde England where minstrels sing in street corners, and troubadours in marketplaces. With the possible exception of King David and Bar Kochva, both of whom were great warriors, all the famous names in Jewish history are those of prophets and teachers who changed the world by utterances of their mouths rather than with their swords and their spears.

Jewish culture *is* boring, shallow and uninspiring. Rather, our distinction and the reason to be Jewish lies in our incomparable God, religion, and values. Smoked-salmon bagels may not have changed the world, but the Jewish Sabbath has. Its goodness has helped bring to the world a holiness that has no parallel. It has become a day of meditation, prayer, and family for the whole world, affording man an awareness that he is more than just an ox that pulls a plough in pursuit of his daily bread. That he is a contemplative, spiritual being who must also cater to the needs of his soul. Moreover, we have given the world a personal God of history who is attentive to human suffering. The idea that all men and women are created in the image of God and are therefore sanctified and equal. The notion of a world run on the principles of law and justice and that man's highest calling is to serve as an agent for their establishment and endless pursuit. Judaism has taught the world about directional history and how all of mankind are slowly progressing toward a world of peace and global fraternity. We have given the world the concept of the nuclear family as the mainstay of society, and the idea of holiness and fidelity in marriage. Judaism gave husbands and wives the *mikveh*, and no better secret for retaining passion in marriage has ever been found. We don our *tefillin* every morning, thereby integrating mind and heart in the service of the divine calling. We affix *mezuzos* to our doors and invite strangers into our homes, thereby transforming them into miniature sanctuaries for the communal good instead of private dwellings designed to keep people out. We may eat Italian or Chinese cuisine, but when we do it is kosher and prepared in a way that cause the animal the least possible pain. And because of the compassion taught us by Judaism, we Jews are the single most charitable community in the world, giving far more charity, percentage-wise, than any other ethnic minority on earth. What is beautiful about us is our religion.

This means that only the Jewish religion has the capacity to instil pride in young Jews. Lox and the novels of Isaac Bashevis Singer are no alternative to prayer in the synagogue, dancing on Simchas Torah, and lighting the menorah on Chanukah. Boris Pasternak, the Jewish convert to Russian orthodoxy, wrote in *Doctor Zhivago*, 'In whose interests is this voluntary martyrdom? Dismiss this army which is forever fighting and being massacred, nobody knows for what.' Yet we do. We have not suffered for ethnicity's sake, but for the glorious light which has had so profound an impact on the world.

Let us have the courage to admit that our culture may not be much to write home about, but that our religion has served as the greatest light to ourselves and other nations throughout history. The book of Deuteronomy declares, 'Moses charged us with the law, as an inheritance for the assembly of Jacob' (33:4). The Jewish faith is the rightful possession of every Jew, and it is incumbent upon Jewish parents to impart this living spring of inspiration to their young. By doing so they will ensure not only that their child remains the next link in an unbroken chain of Jewish existence, but that the child continues the job of serving as an important light in a world suffering from an abundance of darkness.

Man of Technology

But the Jewish man or woman of faith will not cease to be an anachronism, and will not assume their rightful place in society, until their contribution to modern society is re-evaluated and its necessity re-established. There are three principal categories where the man of faith can contribute invaluably toward a world which is fast losing its moral compass.

The first is in the field of depth and human transcendence. Modern man is so concerned with the immediate satiation of his desires and material consumption that he looks at the world in an entirely utilitarian way. When modern man meets a new acquaintance, his first thought is how he might exploit the new relationship to his advantage. Perhaps his new friend has useful business contacts. Or when a man meets an attractive woman, his first thought is how she might eventually service his physical needs. The first thing, there-fore, that the man of faith can do is revisit upon the world a sense of awe, to alert us to the wondrous nature of life, the majesty of God's creation, and the beauty and blessing of human company. The same applies to religion, for the divine nature of religion today loses out to its social dimension and its covenantal role is superseded by its aesthetic value as an adjunct to life. Here the man of faith can reintroduce mankind to God in a holy state of communion, so that religion becomes something experiential rather than just ceremonial.

The second contribution lies in the area of ethics. Without God, modern-day ethics have no anchor and are based solely on human whim. Without an ultimate standard by which to measure right and wrong, good and evil become nothing more than euphemisms for personal or collective tastes. The man and woman of faith can provide a beacon by which humanity can set its moral compass.

The third contribution lies in the realm of crisis. Technological man feels triumphant through his conquering of disease and ability to travel long distances in hours rather than months. In moments of insecurity and fright, however, when he is confronted with a situation that he cannot master, he suddenly finds himself spinning out of control, crying out for an endearing presence who is always attuned to his pain. As the architect of man, God is the only Being capable of understanding man's greatest fears and alleviating his deepest pain. Without God, modern-day man remains a ship tossing in the wind, his cry deafened by the howling tempest, as he becomes lost at sea. The man or woman of faith is the carrier of the religious flame which is the source of all these blessings.

Modern Opportunities

For two thousand years the Jews were cut off from making any direct contribution to wider society, or having any direct impact on it. Christianity and Islam were the dominant religions, and both either persecuted and subdued the Jews directly, or shut them behind ghetto walls. The Jews reacted by strengthening their own identities and developing a philosophy of contempt for their Gentile overlords. Indeed, the immorality and lawlessness which they witnessed and to which they were subject made them despise wider society, and they protected their children from its influences by electing to remain cut off and isolated. Thus was born the idea of a self-imposed ghetto, where Jews voluntarily disengaged from Gentile culture by living among themselves and having little to do with the outside world.

Beginning with the French Revolution and emancipation of European Jewry, all that has changed. Jews are treated as equals of every major society in which they live. Either this acceptance will swallow them whole and lead to their total disappearance, or it will finally present the long-awaited opportunity for the Jews to influence the world at large and live up to the ancient biblical prophecies of the Jews serving as a Light unto the Nations. Today, immersed into a democratic and largely secular society that has become disenchanted with religion, the Jewish faith can finally emerge and have a direct impact on mainstream civilisation. With its strong ethical emphasis, it can serve as an inspiration for modern-day men and women who long for a spirituality which will make them into better people and transform the world into a kinder, gentler place.

This means that Judaism should be promoted, not as a truer or more acceptable religion than all others, but as a model of faith which is capable of reconciling religious ritual with moral imperatives, enabling man to enjoy a strong relationship both with God and with his fellow man. The world cries out for leadership. Judaism is mankind's oldest monotheistic faith. Its light is finally being granted an opportunity to shine.

May its rays illuminate the distant isles, as well as the tiniest crevices of every human heart and soul.

9

Anti-Semitism

Many believe that anti-Semitism has been confined to lower, more illiterate classes. What they forget is that some of the world's most respected thinkers have been rabid anti-Semites. Even moralists like Voltaire, father of the Enlightenment, could not overcome their hatred of the Jews. Voltaire despised the Jews with an intensity that is almost impossible to comprehend. He called Jews, 'the most abominable people in the world', and assessed them in the following way: 'In short, they are a totally ignorant nation who, for many years, have combined contemptible miserliness and the most revolting superstition with a violent hatred of all those nations that have tolerated them. Nevertheless, they should not be burned at the stake.' Asked how Jewish influence could be curbed, the Kantian philosopher Johan Fichte wrote in 1793, 'I see no other way of doing this except to cut off all their heads one night and substitute other heads without a single Jewish thought in them. How shall we defend ourselves against them?'

Jews have also, of course, been hated by other Jews. Karl Marx, for example, was a lifelong anti-Semite who often resorted to Nazi-like invective against the Jews: 'What is the secular cult of the Jew? Haggling. What is his secular god? Money. Well then! Emancipation from haggling and money, from practical, real Judaism would be the self-emancipation of our time …'

Indeed, why anti-Semitism exists with such fervour remains today a great mystery. Traditional academic and social anthropological explanations as to the origin of anti-Semitism – such as the ghost theory, that nobody likes a ghost of a people that should have died out when they were expelled from their land, or the theory that the Jews have been used as scapegoats by totalitarian rulers – cannot account for the lingering hatred of Jews among people of all social classes and religious persuasions, for thousands of years, even in countries where there are no Jews. As David Lloyd George wrote in 1938 in his article, 'What Has the Jew Done?':

> Of all the bigotries that savage the human temper there is none so stupid as anti-Semitism. In the sight of these fanatics, the Jews can do nothing right. If they are rich, they are birds of prey. If they are poor, they are vermin. If they are in favour of war, that is because they want to exploit the bloody feuds of Gentiles to their own profit. If they are anxious for peace, they are either instinctive cowards or traitors. If they give generously – and there are no more liberal givers than the Jews – they are doing it for some selfish purpose of their own. If they don't give, then what would one expect of a Jew?

The Talmud explains how anti-Semitism began and why it has become such a scourge. The ancient rabbis asked, 'Why was Mount Sinai's name called thus? Because from there hatred descended onto the Jews from the nations of the world.' Prior to the Jewish covenant at Mount Sinai, God and His laws were unknown in the world. In this world in which might made right, and the strong vanquished the weak, Judaism was not going to be popular with its message of God looking out for the oppressed and the Ten Commandments' stern prohibitions against theft, adultery and covetousness. Judaism's insistence on the image of God within every human being challenged the accepted ideas of aristocracy, and it has been resisted ever since by those who wished to claim a false superiority.

Hitler treated the war effort against the allies as taking second place to the war against the Jews. Even as his soldiers lay starving on the Eastern and Western fronts, bereft of food, fuel, and ammunition, the railroads continued to ferry Jews to the crematoria of Auschwitz rather than resupply German troops. Holocaust historian Lucy Dawidowicz writes in *The War Against the Jews*:

> Serious people, responsible people, thought that Hitler's notions about the Jews were, at best, merely political bait for disgruntled masses, no more than ideological window dressing to cloak a naked drive for power. Yet precisely the reverse was true. Racial imperialism and the fanatic plan to destroy the Jews were the dominant passions behind the drive for power.

The reason for this is straightforward. The allies represented a temporal problem for Hitler. Today they were his enemies, but tomorrow they might indeed sue for peace and become his allies, as was the case at first with the Soviet Union. But the Jews represented Hitler's eternal, ideological enemies with whom there could only be a struggle to the death.

Hitler sought not only to win the war, but to impose a completely new world order. He saw the complete overturning of the Judeo-Christian ethic. He wanted to return the world to a time in which race theory supplanted the idea of all men having been created in the image of God. He wished to make the world a place where theft, murder, and the evolutionary doctrine of the survival of the fittest replaced the Godly ideas of the sanctity of life and the brotherhood of all mankind. Hitler's first plan, therefore, was to destroy the nation who were witnesses to God in history. If the messengers of good and evil could be removed from the earth, then their message could weaken as well, and perhaps countries like Great Britain might now see the good sense of compromise and cease-fire, even with one so wretched as Hitler.

Reversing Anti-Semitism

Once Elie Wiesel spoke to our students at Oxford and he related how, while he was conversing with the president of an African nation, the president accused the Jews of controlling all the banks and the media. 'No, that is inaccurate,' Wiesel replied. 'We do not, and have not, controlled the world at all. We've played quite a small role in the world up to now. But this is something that I wish the world would allow us to do. I don't want to control the whole world. What I ask is that you give us your children for just one generation, and let us show you what we can teach them. I promise, we will give them back in a better condition than we took them.'

The greatest paradox of anti-Semitism is that it can only be eradicated when the Jews fully live up to their ancient calling and become a light unto the nations. Rabbi Abraham Joshua Heschel, one of the twentieth century's foremost Jewish thinkers wrote, 'The Jews are a messenger who forgot his message.' Only when the Jews impart ethical monotheism to the world, teaching the nations values and ethics – a repugnance of violence and the brotherhood of all mankind – will the earth be rid of senseless, irrational hatred.

This is probably the strongest argument against Jewish insularity. The Jews cannot be perceived as aloof, for this is bound to provoke hostility. Their 'chosenness' is a directive to teach the world the Ten Commandments, rather than a claim to superiority. The Jewish people must refocus their priorities. While combating anti-Semitism is of great significance, the Jews are the nation that cannot shirk the responsibility of the prophets. Judaism must emerge from its hibernation as a pivotal force shaping and influencing the public debate. While the perfection of society is an almost impossible dream, this generation no longer tolerates war, injustice, inequality, the poisoning of our environment, or any of the other evils that were once felt to be inevitable. There is a sudden global change of conscience that seems to be shaking the very roots of our civilisation. More and more, people are coming to the conclusion that the evils of society are diseases that call for a cure. The only thing which is lacking is someone to orchestrate all of the efforts and goodwill together within a divine plan. This is the ancient calling of the Jewish nation: to serve as the trailblazers of religious and ethical consciousness so that the people of the world can join together and create heaven on earth. This is why they are known as the 'chosen people'.

'Becoming a Light unto Nations'

With all the wealth of insights into everyday life which Judaism possesses, the question naturally arises as to why so few non-Jews know anything about Judaism. OK, there aren't that many Jews in the world. But equally, there aren't that many Tibetans, and yet everyone seems to be familiar with the Dalai Lamah. Why did Judaism, with its strong mystical tradition and celebration of everyday life, never become the Buddhism of the Western world, its spirituality embraced by millions of people the world over, even though they are not Jews?

Indeed, given the phenomenal influence which Jews exercise in so many fields of endeavour, the question becomes why have they done so poor a job at promoting Jewish values and teachings? Why has Judaism remained a backwater amidst global Jewish prosperity? With the exception of Maimonides, the world knows nothing of Jewish wise men. Mention names like Akiva, Saadya, Rashi, and Maharal, and you will get blank stares. Why have the Jews been so singularly unsuccessful in conveying the beauty of their own tradition?

The main reason is Jewish insularity, and the cause of Jewish insularity is a basic, if unwitting, contempt for the outside world. The Jews have not affected the world because they have not wanted to, because after centuries of persecution, they have largely ceased to care about the world. Jews are not racists, but while they do not look down on non-Jews, they look down on non-Jewish living and non-Jewish society. That is why we have always insulated ourselves from it.

Throughout the world, wherever Jews dwell, notwithstanding the success we have attained in commerce and the professions, we still lead mostly insular lives. Jews live in self-imposed ghettos amongst themselves. A classic case in point is the Golders Green area in north-west London where over sixty per cent of all British Jews today reside. Jews do not congregate together for communal or security reasons alone, but also because they feel that non-Jewish society is ultimately incapable of being redeemed.

Jews use the word goy, or Gentile, not to connote any racist dislike of non-Jews. Rather, it is a pejorative term which hints at a certain lack of spiritual or moral sophistication, yobbery and bummishness. Goishe society refers to the social mores of the street, of the lager louts and football hooligans, the kind of rowdy and uncouth behaviour that Jews could never see themselves a part of. In fact, many Jews are always sitting around waiting for the brute in the Gentile to be manifest. After so many centuries of anti-Semitism, many Jews believe that Jew-hatred is always lurking just beneath the surface of what appears to be civilised Gentile society.

Jewish insularity and their shirking of their ancient responsibility of trying to raise the world to a higher spiritual plane through direct interaction with the world around them are largely due to the negative Jewish view of Gentile culture. This is not a criticism on my part against the Jewish community. Indeed one might say that the nations of the world have justly earned the scorn of the Jewish people. At one point or another they have been expelled from nearly every country of residence in the most cruel of ways, despite the impressive contributions they made to their host nations. Why should the Jews desire to help them redeem themselves? Cocooning oneself and abandoning the world to its own devices seems a natural response. But times have changed drastically. For the first time in its history, the Jewish nation has been afforded an opportunity to bring the light of Godliness and goodness to the world. Dare we forsake it?

European Anti-Semitism

I am especially amazed at the degree to which European Jews believe that anti-Semitism animates so much of the world. I remember having lunch with a prominent Anglo-Jewish businessman. He counts among his friends all the leading lights of business and politics. Still, he once said to me that if a Hitler were to emerge in Britain, he couldn't see any of his non-Jewish colleagues coming to the rescue of his family.

But what evidence do we Jews have that the enlightened nations of the western world continue to be anti-Semitic? Some will, for example, cite the bias against Israel on the part of the British media. Most British media outlets do not give Israel a fair deal. I do not, however, believe that this is due to anti-Semitism, but rather to the traditional British support for the underdog. And, anyway, the State of Israel's PR is so bad that somehow they have allowed the one hundred and twenty million oil-rich Arabs who encircle them to manoeuvre themselves into a position where they are perceived as victims in an expansionist war waged by four million Jews. While this perception is ludicrously mistaken, it does not constitute anti-Semitism.

Like many Jews, up until two years ago I was convinced that Poles were overwhelmingly anti-Semitic. But when I was escorted to Poland by my good friend Jonathan Webber, we came to a small village not far from the legendary *shtetl* of Belz. He asked an elderly gentleman in Polish as to the whereabouts of the old Jewish cemetery. The man put his head into the window of our car, pointed in the direction of a field grown over with shrubs and vines. Jonathan translated as the man told of us how he remembers when the pretty little Jewish girl, who was his next-door neighbour in the village, was taken away from her home by the German soldiers one morning, lined up with the other Jews of the village, and shot in the back. He wept uncontrollably as he told the story. I saw many similar displays of emotion that day when other Poles recounted to us how their Jewish neighbours were slaughtered.

Does this mean that there weren't many Poles who didn't dance for joy upon witnessing the extermination of the Jews? Of course not. For hundreds of years the Poles were generally anti-Semitic. What it does mean is that while we must always remember the suffering of our brethren throughout history, and hate the perpetrators of these barbaric acts, we must also remember that this current generation is not the one responsible for them. People can and do change and we must not allow our suffering at the hands of barbaric generations of Gentiles to taint our perception of our contemporary non-Jewish colleagues.

When the L'Chaim Society recently hosted the German Ambassador to the United Kingdom, one of my close friends called me and asked, 'How can you open your home to a Nazi?' My protestations that this Ambassador was a friend of the Jews and had absolutely nothing to do with the holocaust, fell on deaf ears. Yet we do well to remember that our Torah does not believe in the transmission of sin across generations. Jewish teaching advocates personal accountability but it strongly rejects vertical responsibility. The Germans who murdered six million innocent Jews were the parents of today's Germans. While their children must do everything in their power to remember those terrible events and try and understand what could have led their parents to become monsters, they are still under no obligation to repent for, or to suffer scorn over, their parent's actions – so long as they condemn their inhuman actions and show their extravagant love for the Jewish nation. Jewish antipathy toward the younger generation of Germans is not only misguided, but constitutes a shirking of our Biblical obligation to radiate Godly light and love to the earth's inhabitants, bringing them closer to their Father in heaven.

Gaining Pride in Our Tradition

Personally, I am in a unique position to judge the attitude with which the Jewish world approaches the non-Jewish world. The L'Chaim Society which I founded eleven years ago in Oxford became the first ever Jewish organisation with a significant non-Jewish membership. We have also had many non-Jewish officers, including African-Americans, Blacks, Mormons, atheists and fundamentalist Christians. By the fourth year of its operation, the L'Chaim Society already had over one thousand non-Jewish members. We were proud of this fact and promoted it widely. We felt that we were creating a model of a community in which young adults of different faiths could come together, without softening their respective identities. But it created an unbelievable uproar both in the Anglo-Jewish community and abroad. I was accosted by religious and secular Jewish parents wherever I went. 'Why are you bringing non-Jews to Jewish events? Are you encouraging inter-marriage?' 'I won't let my daughter go to you. I didn't send her to Oxford to meet a non-Jewish husband over the Sabbath dinner table.' After every lecture, the first question demanded an answer why the L'Chaim Society allowed non-Jewish membership of the organisation.

The rejection of the non-Jewish world in the thought that insularity will safeguard the future of the Jewish nation is a misguided and mistaken policy which is bound to backfire. On the contrary, in an open and egalitarian society, it will lead young Jewish men and women to want to rebel. The way that a wife ensures the fidelity of her husband is not by locking him in a closet, but by engendering within him a feeling of love and commitment. Similarly, the way that Jews ensure the future of the Jewish nation is by causing young Jews to internalise their Jewish commitment so that it accompanies them in every place and predicament. A Jewish man should seek to marry a Jewish woman because he wishes to perpetuate his people and their legacy, and not because there simply were no other women around to marry. And the strongest means by which to instil a sense of Jewishness in today's young, is to give them pride in their tradition.

There is no better way to teach people to love a tradition than to get them to teach and serve as exponents of that tradition. If young Jews today felt that they had an ancient calling as part of a Godly people to make the world a better place – if they felt that they had a certain spiritual light to radiate to the world – they would rush to embrace their tradition with great pride because they would see its effects on the larger society. But when people are told only to insulate themselves on behalf of what seems to them a meaningless tradition which benefits naught but them, when Judaism is portrayed as a tradition that demands limitless sacrifice with comparatively little social gain, the Jewish faith is sure to suffer.

I am a Jewish universalist. I believe that the Jewish nation has lost its way whenever its highest objective becomes the preservation of its own heritage with no consideration as to how that heritage – bringing man closer to his fellow man and his Creator – is influencing the wider world. I have no desire to preserve a nation which has no other objective than ensuring its own survival. Young Jews hear their parents pressuring them to marry Jewish because they want to have Jewish grandchildren. When the children ask, what difference does that make to you since you ignore every other tenet of the faith, they are stumped into silence. But inconsistency seldom motivates young people to emulate the example of their parents. Parents must lead by example.

Reaching Out to Other Religions

Jews can no longer adopt the attitude of 'who cares what happens to the non-Jewish world as long as the Jewish nation is still strong'. We must overcome our collective scarring over thousands of years and learn that the time has come to open our hearts fully to working with non-Jewish religions. Although Christianity, for example, was the enemy of Jews and Judaism for nearly two millennia, in this respect times have now significantly changed as well. There is a Pope who has granted diplomatic recognition to the State of Israel, and Christian fundamentalists in the United States represent some of Israel's most trusted allies.

Jews must reach out to Christians and especially to the considerable overtures being made by many of the Christian clergy in pursuit of a policy of reconciliation with their Jewish brethren. Whatever pain has been inflicted upon the Jews through non-Jewish atrocities must today be seen as something of the past. To be sure, we must always be vigilant and protect ourselves from outbursts of anti-Semitism. But the post-Holocaust generation is the first Jewish generation of all time who truly have an opportunity to establish the Jewish voice as a dynamic and influential force within society which helps to shape public debate. It would be a tragedy to squander that opportunity because we are still haunted by the ghosts of our past.

Like a country with an outdated foreign policy which has not been revised since the end of the cold war, the Jews continue to insist that combating anti-Semitism is the most important Jewish prerogative. Similarly, many Jews believe, that deep-down all Gentiles harbour anti-Semitism. While, of course, at times this can be true, it can sometimes be like the case of the Jewish man with a stutter who went for an interview to be a radio presenter and accused the management of anti-Semitism when he did not get the job. The ongoing fear of latent anti-Semitism is one of the main reasons why so many young Jews in Oxford hide their Jewish identity. They wear yarmulkas at home, but will immediately take them off upon arriving at the university, fearing that they will be treated with prejudice and receive worse exam results than they ought to. In each case my response to them is the same: 'Blame your failures on yourself, not on someone else.'

Teaching young Jews to be scared of who they are impedes them from taking their rightful place among the nations. Yet fear is employed in an effort to ensure the continuity of the Jewish people. Indeed, the saying in Jewish communal work goes, 'There's no business like *Shoah*-business' (*Shoah* meaning Holocaust). The Holocaust is bandied around by many Jewish organisation because they know that it is an emotive enough subject to induce Jews to act. It pulls all the right heart strings and is guaranteed to overcome Jewish apathy. But there is a better way of going about things. Judaism and Jewish identity are sufficiently glorious that we can motivate the younger generation to embrace them out of love rather than fear.

Continuing to raise Jewish children in the belief that they will always be hated and should always be on their guard is incredibly destructive. Not only will it preclude them from having sufficient self-confidence – since they think that they will never get a fair chance. It will also guarantee that they hide their Jewishness and become ashamed of who they are. This does not mean that, at times, anti-Semitism does not exist. What it does mean is that the fear that it pervades society *in general* is far more destructive to the Jews than anyone else.

Our Ancient Calling

It is profoundly saddening that, in this age of egalitarian principle, so many Jews feel uncomfortable with being the chosen nation to the point where they actively deny it. As Thomas Sewell, the noted black economist writes, 'Even when the Jews lived in slums, they were slums with a differ-ence – lower alcoholism, homicide, accidental death rates than other slums, or even the city as a whole. Their children had lower truancy rates, lower juvenile delinquency rates, and (by the 1930s) higher IQs than other children ... Despite a voluminous literature claiming that slums shape people's values, the Jews had their own values, and they took those values into and out of the slums.'

The Jewish penchant for study could do so much to focus the modern world away from television and back to literacy and books. In their excellent book, *Why the Jews?*, Dennis Prager and Joseph Telushki quote the letter of an Egyptian Jewish woman written in the twelfth century on her death-bed: 'I tell you my sister … that I have fallen into a grievous disease and there is little possibility of recovering from it … If the Lord on High should decree my death, my greatest wish is that you should take care of my little daughter and make an effort for her to study. Indeed, I know that I am imposing a heavy burden on you. For we do not have the wherewithal for her upkeep, let alone the cost of tuition. But we have an example from our mother and teacher, the servant of the Lord.' As the historian Haim Hillel BenSasson has concluded, 'Here is an instance of a Jewish family that was certainly not well-to-do in which the women of two genera-tions were educated and saw to the education of their daughters.' Jews have always believed that study was sacred and put enormous emphasis on education. This may account for the fact that 27 per cent of American Nobel prize winners are Jewish and that American Jews are twice as likely as non-Jews to go to College.

Similarly, the Jews have always been the most charitable by far of any ethnic minority. Anti-Semites throughout the ages have always charged the Jews with being excessively wealthy. This is preposterous. Up until modern times, Jews were a despised and poor minority who only had the sem-blance of wealth because of their extraordinary autonomous social services. Because Jews always looked after their poor, it appeared as though the Jews had no one in need of clothing or shoes.

For example, among the few thousand Jews living in seventeenth-century Rome, seven charitable societies pro-vided clothes, shoes, linen, and beds for the poor. Two other societies provided trousseaus for poor brides, another aided families struck by a sudden death, and yet another was responsible for visiting the sick. One special society collected charity for Jews in Israel, and another eleven groups raised money for Jewish educational and religious institutions. One particularly dramatic, though not atypical, example of Jewish philanthropy, cited by Chaim Bermant, was in London in the early nineteenth century where almost half the Jewish population was supported by the other half. This explains why large Jewish charities, like the United Jewish Appeal in the United States, and Jewish Care and the United Jewish Israel Appeal in Britain, rank among the top ten charities in their respective countries, even though the Jews are less than two per cent of the population in the United States, and less than one per cent in Britain.

In a world witnessing the highest divorce rates ever and the crumbling of the nuclear family, the Jews provide an outstanding example of family and marriage. Think about it. In *The Republic*, Plato advocated the abandonment of the nuclear family in favour of friendship since 'Friends have all things in common.' Similarly, Lycurgus, formulator of the Spartan constitution, decreed that Spartans should give 'their wives to whom they should think fit, so that they might have children by them.' Even Christianity idealised non-family life in the epistles of Paul: 'It is well for a man not to touch a woman. But because of the temptation to immorality, each man should have his own wife … I say this by way of confession, not of command. I wish that all were [celibate] as I myself am' (Cor. 7:1-7).

But the ancient rabbis of the Talmud taught that one of the first things asked of a soul in judgement after its time on the earth is, 'Did you fulfil your duty with regard to establishing a family?' A man could not become the Jewish High Priest unless he was married, and could not be a judge of the Sanhedrin, the Jewish high court, unless he had children 'since they teach him compassion.' There are countless other examples of how much the Jews may impart to the world. The Jewish people are the chosen nation; chosen to teach the world about God and goodness and to serve as a light unto the nations. We must carry that responsibility with pride and humility and work with our non-Jewish brothers to create heaven on earth.

Judaism as the Next Buddhism

Today we have the most glorious opportunity of all time as Jews. We can finally rid ourselves of fear, come out of our cocoon, our self-imposed ghettos, and establish Judaism and Jewish spirituality as one of the greatest lights the world has ever seen. I believe that in the coming century Judaism will emerge as the next Buddhism, a religion which the West's inhabitants do not directly adopt, but look to as the source for their own spirituality. With its constant emphasis on the need for synthesis between body and soul, heaven and earth, Judaism is uniquely qualified to guide the spiritual lives of today's young men and women who want to achieve great professional success, without suffocating their souls in the process.

Over the past few centuries, the world underwent three great phases. The first was the Christian wave, which was a commitment to material withdrawal and sensual repression. The second wave was the atheistic explosion which began with Darwin in the 1860's, and lasted for about a century. This was a time of rebellion from religion and material and sensual indulgence. The backlash to this Godlessness brought on the third great wave, in which young Westerners turned in huge number to eastern religions and meditation as a reaction to the vacuous consumerism which was supposed to make them happy. All these experiments ultimately failed.

Judaism enjoins man, however, not to leave the earth and connect with God in heaven, but to create heaven on earth. Not to renounce material pleasures, but to celebrate our humanity with God as our partner. Not to embrace a life of celibacy, but of holiness in sexual relations. Only Judaism emphasises that body and soul can achieve a perfect harmony, and that man can do good by harnessing, rather than transcending, his most basic instincts. Judaism is the perfect spiritual energy for a generation that wants to be wealthier and more prosperous than ever before, but also not to be seduced by its own prosperity. Judaism teaches man to embrace God with every fibre of his nature. This does not mean that our religion is any better than others. Only that the opportunity has finally come for our religion to reveal its teachings to an increasingly willing audience.

10

Religion in Action

The Jew believes in the earth as a hallowed part of creation and affirms that the divine image is imprinted on every human. This means that Judaism celebrates hard action. Where the Christian speaks of love, the Jew says that there can be no love without justice, and thus preserves the law. This downward orientation of bringing God into the world as the focal point of the religion spawns the following central tenets of Judaism:

1. *Revelation and prophecy*. Judaism is about God coming down to man and revealing how He may be approached rather than man merely theorising about what would make the deity happy. Judaism is not a religion of the philosopher but of the revelationist. What is important is to *serve* God rather than *understand* Him. The most central moment in the Jewish religion was the revelation of God at the foot of Mount Sinai to the collective House of Israel just weeks after they had emerged from Egyptian slavery. Other world religions, most notably Christianity, place their emphasis on dogmatic theology, whereby man exercises his mind to its uttermost limits in an effort to understand God's mysteries. They emphasise the comprehension of God within the eye of the mind. Judaism, however, stresses the apprehension of the deity through Godly works. Judaism is experiential, as op-

posed to philosophical. It is a religion of action wherein God is captured through a Godly deed.

2. *Physical objects in religious worship*. Judaism has been much maligned by other religious thinkers – St Paul in his epistles springs immediately to mind – as being burdened and overrun by a concern for the minutiae of life, rather than focusing on the service of God through faith. 'For if a person could achieve salvation through good works [the law], then Christ would have died in vain' (Gal. 2:21). Similarly, '… we conclude that a man is put right with God only through faith and not by doing what the law commands' (Rom. 3:28). But Judaism believes that good deeds are far more important than faith.

Judaism worships God with a plethora of physical objects but the use of these material objects in religious ritual and the vast scope of Jewish law derive from Judaism's obsession with consecrating the earth. The Jew is charged with bringing the very dust of creation into the camp of holiness. Judaism is not concerned with creating little sanctuaries of Godliness, but rather with uplifting all the earth to a higher spiritual plane. Therefore, a Jew must dispel the notion which ascribes holiness to the synagogue and the church, but not to the marketplace or the bedroom. This kind of spiritual compart-mentalisation is wholly foreign to Judaism. From a Jewish perspective, the street is as holy as the basilica – each provides an opportunity to create a sepulchre of sanctity.

Thus, there are as many laws regarding behaviour in the street as there are for the synagogue; and as many laws regulating lovemaking in the bedroom as ethics in the board-room. The operative mode of thought in Judaism is that the absence of God from our physical world is nothing but an illusion. As an inscription found on the wall of a cellar in Cologne, Germany, where Jews hid from the Nazis, read, 'I believe in the sun even when it is not shining. I believe in love even when not feeling it. I believe in God even when He is silent.' God hides behind the veneer of nature. Miracles are not a sudden intervention of God in the laws of nature. Rather, these laws are themselves upheld by God at every instant. The only thing distinguishing nature from miracle is the degree of regularity. If the Red Sea were to part every day at precisely 3:30 p.m. we would dismiss this as a natural occurrence. Man's purpose is to make the invisible God a visible and potent force throughout society. Just because it appears as though God resides in the holy man more than the peasant, does not make it so. Rather, both are born with a Godly soul and with inherent holy potential. The goal is to translate that potential into the actual, so that the Almighty is manifest is every atom of His creation.

3. *Action as opposed to meditation.* In other religions, notably Hinduism and Buddhism, the emphasis is on personal enlightenment. A world of cerebral thought, the inner world of man, is seen as superior to the external reality with its corruption and darkness. Man is bidden to withdraw into a world in which he escapes the gore of everyday life by appealing to his higher senses and faculties, ultimately achieving expiation of self and nirvana. Christianity, with its emphasis on the primacy of faith, is similar. In Judaism, however, the purpose of man is not to be defeated, or to escape the darkness of the world. Rather, he must seek to enlighten not himself so much as the world around him. By bringing God into our world and promoting love and justice,

we bring supernal light, a Godly freshness that brightens the world and cures it of a putrid air of suffocating selfishness.

4. *World redemption precedes personal salvation.* Since other religions disdain physical existence, there is no real emphasis on the need for man to establish love and justice in this world as an end in itself. Rather, the emphasis is on personal salvation. In other religions, man's purpose in bettering the world is primarily so that he will not be corrupted by an unholy environment. But principally, the objective is inner, as opposed to outer, perfection. By practising acts of kindness, man inherits a place in the eternal world. Religion is thus viewed as essentially an individual and personal endeavour. In Judaism, however, the ultimate purpose of existence is to redeem the collective world.

The pursuit of love and justice are ends in themselves, irrespective of their effect on man. Making the world a better place is the highest religious calling. Therefore, even if man gives charity for the wrong reasons – to see his name up in lights or to receive a knighthood – he is still vastly praiseworthy, since the condition of the world precedes the state of his soul. Every action that brings goodness to the world is good in an unqualified sense, even when impelled by imperfect motivation.

Central to Judaism is the belief in the coming of the Messiah, a time in which God's light will shine openly in the world. The Jewish apocalyptic vision is of an eternal era of peace and brotherhood on this earth, rather than in the heavens. When a Jew speaks of the world-to-come, he means this world the way it will be when it is perfected. But he is still talking about the physical earth. The purpose of the Jew is to establish God as a tangible reality in the physical world, thereby re-enacting the easy harmony which once existed between heaven and earth. The Jew rejects mind/matter, body/soul, and heaven/earth dualism, in favour of an all-encompassing monism. God's light envelops the whole of creation. As the sun lights up the earth, God illuminates the cosmos. By using physical objects, which lack overt spirituality, in the worship of God, the Jew re-establishes the perimeter of holiness as encompassing all of material creation.

5. *The sublimeness of the everyday.* Judaism celebrates the everyday aspects of life, rather than the great miracles of the past, and the faith of the simple man in the street, above the martyrdom of saints. It is, after all, the little hello and good-bye kisses between husband and wife which account for the most meaningful part of every relationship. The Jew delivers over to God not only his overtly spiritual aspects – his faith, his charity, his goodness – but even those things which have no overt religious content, like his business affairs, his sex life, his professional aspirations, and his material wealth. The religious man or woman of faith is expected to deliver over to God all of themselves and not just the grander aspects of their being. If you love someone, you love all of them, and when you hug someone, you embrace their non-descript part, like their back.

Judaism understood from the start that real service of God involves two things: first, a wholehearted acceptance of the will of God, and allowing Him to set the agenda of how He wishes to be approached. Second, real service of God, and ultimately the measure of every relationship, is found in the details, rather than just the big plan. A wife asks her husband to take her to see *Evita* for her birthday. Instead, he takes her to see *The Texas Chainsaw Massacre*, and justifies his action by thinking that the important thing is that he made time for his wife for her birthday and took her out. The details aren't important. Where he took her is not as important as the fact that he showed his love and devotion by making a special evening of her birthday. But all she feels is anger and exploitation. The fact that he is inattentive to the details of her requests shows her that he does not take her or her will seriously. He leaves himself the latitude to interpret her requests, thereby inadvertently treating her like a child or someone senile.

6. *Law*. In Christianity the purpose of the gospel is to convey to man the core teachings of Jesus, God the Son, and how he lived. In Judaism, the purpose of the scripture is to teach us, not so much about God – there is precious little about God's being in the Torah – but rather about ourselves and how we might live Godly lives. The Jewish Bible is a book about man and a history of how he struggled in his developing relationship with God. Thus, law, or precise rules of how we must live and behave, are central to the Jewish religion. St Paul always attacked the law as an impediment to righteousness: 'Therefore no one will be declared righteous in his sight by observing the law; rather, through the law we become conscious of sin. But now a righteousness from God, apart from law, has been made known, to which the law and the Prophets testify.' (Rom. 3:20-21). But to the Jews, divine law constitutes the channels of communication – the most highly tuned frequency – by which man can always apprehend God. Far from suppressing our religious spirit, the law focuses and harnesses it. If we are to establish a relationship with God and make Him a part of our world, then we must accommodate

His will. In Judaism, the laws of the Torah are a revelation of the divine will, and observance of them establishes a loving relationship between Creator and creature.

7. *The Sabbath.* When Adam and Eve sinned in the Garden of Eden, the special light of truth which radiated throughout the world in the original seven days of creation became hidden. Suddenly, the world was shrouded in darkness, itself obscuring the reality of its origin. Rather than serving as His graffiti, the world became God's mask. In only one time and one place did God's light remain burning brightly: the time was the Sabbath day, the place was the Holy Land of Israel. Since time and space are the very matrix of material existence, it is the objective of the Jew to elevate and raise both these components to holiness. God Himself began by making one day and one place holy, and enjoined man to continue the process.

The objective of the Jew is to make more times and more places holy, until all the earth once again shines with spiritual light. The week is structured in such a way that even if the Jew remains completely stationary and idle, every seven days he is overtaken by the spirit of the Sabbath which beckons him to make the other weekdays holy as well. Thus, when Jewish parents play with their children during the week, they cordon off this special and holy moment so that nothing can intrude, much in the same way that we refrain from answering the phone on the Sabbath. The Jew extrapolates beyond the confines of the holy Shabbos day and imports its sanctity to every weekday endeavour, so that God is his partner in all ways and in all things.

11

Cornerstones of Civilisation

Western civilisation is predicated on various foundation stones. As a general introduction to some of the themes that are found in this book, I list below the eighteen cardinal tenets of our modern civilisation, and how each emanates from a different strand within the fabric of the Bible and the Jewish faith. Indeed, Judaism may be described as a programme of action aimed at instilling these values within society and man.

1. The belief in the *brotherhood of mankind* and the kinship of all living things. This belief is predicated on the understanding that we all ultimately emanate from a single source in God, and that thus humanity is one family who are responsible for one another. Because we are all children of the one God, there is hope that all mankind can live together in peace and harmony with each other. There is no dualism, or two powers, who are responsible for existence. God is the Master of the universe. Evil is therefore always weaker than good, and benevolent forces will always triumph over darkness. There is an all-encompassing unity at the heart of creation. There are no opposing forces at odds in the universe.

2. The belief in the *equality* of all mankind and that humans have a dignity and uniqueness which must be upheld and protected by all their human counterparts. Every human is

special and irreplaceable. Man's worth is not judged by possessions acquired, but by the infinite holy soul possessed within his bosom. Human life is not just valuable but sacred. All this stems from the biblical statement that man was created in the image of God.

3. *History is directional* and continually evolves for the betterment of mankind. Every good deed, however small, is significant and cumulative, and ultimately brings us closer to the perfect world which we have in our power to bring upon us. Action is far more significant than dogma or belief. The right thing should be done even for the wrong reasons. This springs from the ancient Jewish belief in the Messiah, who will one day put the finishing touches on perfecting the world, and the centrality of *mitzvot* to Jewish tradition.

4. *Peace is superior to war*, and forgiveness higher than vengeance. Cultivating our minds in study is far more noble than cultivating our bodies. This stems from the Jewish insistence that the Sabbath, a day of rest, is holier than all the work days of the week, as well as from the ancient Messianic prophecies which promised a perfect world devoid of conflict and hostilities.

5. *Man is utterly free*. Empowered with freedom of choice, he is capable of liberating himself from the cage of human nature. There is no fate, neither in the stars, nor in our genes. Every man and woman are accountable for their actions and shall be rewarded for the good and punished for the evil which they practise. Man is not an animal, and is therefore always in control of his own destiny. This idea flows from the festival of Passover and the exodus from Egypt, which

emphasises that the Jew has been permanently and irrevocably redeemed from Egypt, the symbol of human limitations.

6. *The law is ineffective unless it is immutable.* Morality and ethics must be anchored in an absolute divine standard. Law is the basis for every relationship since everything needs rules of engagement. There is a universal standard of conduct by which all people must treat each other. Law is the best means by which to communicate love. While man possesses good, he cannot be trusted as the arbiter of his own morality. Law does not stultify. Rather, it focuses our potential and translates it into the actual. Any society not based on the dictates of law is unjust. There is no moral relativism at work in creation, but rather God's law represents the noblest ideals of goodness. This crucial concept arises out of the Ten Commandments and the festival of Shavuot wherein the law was given by God at Sinai.

7. *Man is custodian of the earth* and the world is his garden which he must nurture and protect. Man is not master of the planet, but must seek to be one with the universe, protecting all life, along with his environment. Sadistic treatment of animals, or abuse of the environment, is a grave sin which will result in man's being driven from the earth. This idea emanates from Adam and Eve's having been placed in the Garden of Eden, as well as from the festival of Sukkot, a time for man's regular and total immersion in nature.

8. *Leadership is the cornerstone of human inspiration and social change.* Strong leadership is central to every healthy society. This concept emerges from the centrality of the Messiah to social change, as well as the critical role which

the rabbis, prophets and priests have always played in Jewish history.

9. Man must have *values* by which he lives. A healthy life is one in which priorities are set. Those things, like family, which are eternal and valuable, must be placed before the ephemeral and superficial, like career and success. The important must always precede the urgent. A day of rest every week is essential in retreating from the noise and bustle of everyday life in order to reconsider priorities and rejuvenate the spirit. Indeed, Judaism is solely responsible for teaching man that rest has a higher function than simply facilitating more work. This is another idea which stems from the weekly Sabbath, a day which cannot be compromised for commerce or financial gain. The Sabbath is an uninterrupted celebration of values.

10. *Man can always repent and start anew.* He possesses an internal soul which transcends the negative things he does. He is not merely the sum total of his actions. Renewal is at the heart of retaining passion in life, and man is possessed of an infinite internal capacity to achieve this aim. This idea stems from the Jewish belief in repentance and the numerous biblical examples of God heartily accepting sincere regret, most notably in the story of the prophet Jonah and the city of Nineveh. It is also the theme behind the Jewish New Year, Rosh Hashana and the Jewish Day of Atonement, Yom Kippur.

11. *Man must harbour a hatred for war, violence, and the sight of blood.* Instilling these ideas is the whole purpose behind the Jewish dietary laws of kashrut and prohibitions of eating blood.

12. *The family is the bedrock of society* and the most important social unit. Some of the most important biblical observances, such as the eating of the Paschal lamb, can only be done by family. Similarly, the Bible always counts the Jewish people in denominations of tribe and family, and all the major Jewish festivals were designed as a time for the congregation of the community and the family.

13. *Humans must never accept the suffering of their fellow men in silence.* Man need not bow his head in submission in the face of seeming divine injustice. Rather, man's highest calling is wrestling with God, which involves fighting disease, preventing disasters, prolonging life, etc. Men and women are invited to enter into a real relationship with God, involving give and take, and not merely to bow and submit. This idea, found only in Judaism, traces its origin to the name Israel, which translates as 'he who wrestles with God', as well as to the great giants of Jewish history, like Abraham and Moses, who wrestled with God to refrain from punishing sinners.

14. *Men and women are different but equal.* Each has different ways by which to maximise their fullest, unique potentials. This stems from Adam and Eve having been created separately, but complementing each other. They are described as each other's help-mates. The Bible gives different laws for men and women, both of which are vital to the maximisation of their potential.

15. *The world is enriched by cultural diversity*, rather than being one homogeneous whole or indistinguishable morass. Racism is evil because it denies the enrichment that every

people brings as it joins the family of nations. By working together, respecting one another, and learning from each other's differences, we create a family of nations, or to use the biblical metaphor, a garden whose beauty is dependent on its different colours and fauna. This critical idea, which the world has only recently begun to appreciate, is inherent in the idea of the Jews being the nation chosen to bring together the disparate contributions of all other nations within one divine framework. The participation of each individual is crucial to the realisation of the divine plan.

16. *The most beautiful things in life are those which, like love, hope and faith, are transcendent* and cannot be experienced with the five senses. This follows from the belief in God and spirituality. The Jews were commanded to put their faith in God's invisible being before all things. Delaying the gratification of the senses in an effort to live by divine dictate is the essence of religious commitment.

17. *Man must do the right thing because it is right*, even if it makes him deeply unpopular. This, one of man's hardest lessons, has been taught to the Jews by two thousand years of anti-Semitism. The high moral standards which the Jews undertook at Sinai made them the conscience of the world and deeply unpopular.

18. *Doing the right thing for the wrong reasons* is far more important than refraining until we develop the proper motivation. Actions speak louder than thoughts or words. This idea is based on the Jewish obsession with world redemption, which always supersedes personal salvation.

12

The Future of the Diaspora

Like most dormant Jewish communities, British Jewry is a society blessed with many virtues, not least of which is one of the most developed and best supported Jewish social services network in the world. Indeed, we have much to be proud of. But that does not change the basic fact that its community is dwindling fast. Intermarriage is up higher than ever before, and a terrible rot, born of cynicism and virtual civil war between orthodoxy and reform, is eroding our hope for the future.

In particular, there are two vital areas in which we as a community have failed. The first is the art of renewal. Novel ideas and new methods of bringing in disinterested and disaffected communal members are simply not being put forward. Which brings us to the second failure. Even if novel and exciting ideas are introduced, Anglo-Jewry has a wonderful knack of killing them dead in the water.

We lack the courage and conviction to implement such ideas, especially if they are given the ultimate insult in communal lingo, namely, if they are perceived as 'controversial'. Like all small communities, Anglo-Jewry has a visceral dislike of anything remotely innovative, fearing it might bring the structure down. It prefers instead the safety of accepted communal norms, even when such protocols are hopelessly outdated.

But the unique challenges of our age call for bold new

initiatives. Many will say that our community is not so bad, and there is nothing wrong with playing second fiddle to Israel or American Jewry. But I believe that the time has come for us to stop being satisfied with third best. Anglo-Jewry should today aspire to global Jewish leadership by having the courage to implement a bold new vision.

There is a particular problem with the Anglo-Jewish syna-gogue. Having run the L'Chaim Society in Oxford for eleven years, I have seen first-hand the effects of not having a strong synagogue service which is the central point in building any community. L'Chaim has had, and continues to run, fantastic weekly programmes. But because we do not have a syna-gogue into which to funnel our new-found adherents we have never had the good fortune of building a permanent commu-nity. Thus, like so many other Jewish outreach organisations, we have seen the effects of pumping people up with novel and exciting ideas, only to watch them gradually cool off for lack of follow-up. And follow-up means a regular commu-nity revolving around a house of prayer, where people of all ages and from all walks of life can come together and meet new and old friends on a regular basis in the synagogue.

But, on the whole, our synagogues in Britain are stultify-ingly boring. Of the congregants who come regularly to synagogue, some fight off slumber, while others sink into a deep coma. Others are prepared to remain awake in the hope of hearing the latest *shule* politics or having the unique privilege of hearing the rabbi criticise someone from the pulpit. The following is a list of ideas which I believe are fundamental if our synagogues and communities are to enjoy an immediate renaissance.

1. The synagogue service ought be radically redesigned. The

age of the large, cathedral-like synagogue, filled with a melodious cantor and accompanying choir, is over. Our *Shules* are too large and impersonal. The modern age is one characterised above all else by a need for (a) participation, and (b) personal attention. We need to sacrifice the grandeur of the cathedrals of old and give way to the *shtiebel*-like intimacy of the new era if the *shule* is to become an inviting home for the young. Our *shules* must be made to resemble *shtiebels* that draw in the individual congregant and make him or her feel like a participant rather than a detached observer. A warm, intimate environment should be created, meaning that the one large synagogue for the whole neighbourhood should be downsized into several smaller synagogues.

2. Synagogue services should cease being a spectator sport. The great rages of our age are not radio programmes with exciting presenters, but rather radio call-in shows and tv shows where people can tell their opinion and their life-story. This is why the choirs should be abolished. Because they do the singing for you. People want to hear their own voices, they want to participate. Anglo-Jewish choirs are beautiful. But if people want a concert they can go to a centre for the arts. Young people are unmoved by a choir's lengthy *chazanut*. Ridding the *shule* of the choir means that the service should be cut down and last, on Shabbos morning, for no longer than two hours. The same applies to the prayer service. The *davening* should be focused on making people understand what they are saying, so that the rabbi takes a far more active role in leading the prayer services than the *Chazzan*. While there should not be any modification in our beautiful and ancient prayer liturgy, there should be a short

explanation of the prayers at several key points in the service, and there should be a short overview of the weekly reading at the beginning of the *Sidra*, weekly Bible readings, and an even shorter one before each individual *aliyah*, section of the readings, so that people can derive inspiration from the all-important weekly reading of the Torah.

3. At the conclusion of the service, the congregation should be seated, texts should be distributed, and there should be a proper class given by the rabbi in place of, or in addition to, the sermon. Sermons provide inspiration, but they do not allow the congregation to participate, offer insights, and ask questions. A rabbi's pre-eminent role should be teaching rather than preaching. With the prayer service reduced to one hundred and twenty minutes, this affords the rabbi a very respectable forty five minutes to truly educate his congregation in a traditional Jewish text, or in the finer points of the Parsha of the week, when the services are over. The congregation should be drawn into real study, in which they have the opportunity to offer their own insights and be stimulated to pick up a book when they return home, rather than feel Jewishly satiated until the next Shabbos. In short, the *shule* should be transformed from a *beis knesset*, house of congregation, to a *beis midrash*, house of study, which stimulates and engages the congregants.

When the class is concluded, the congregation deserve to be rewarded for all their efforts. What they should receive now is the most wonderful *kiddush*. Ours is, thank God, the most prosperous, wealthiest, Jewish generation of all time. At home we want nothing but the best, and we spend a small fortune entertaining our friends at dinner parties. Every communal charity dinner must have the best caterer if money is to be raised. So why is it that weekly *kiddush* at *shule* offers last year's biscuits, and sweet *kiddush* wine, which is far better suited to being used as a pesticide at home, rather than as a beverage in *shule*? It is nothing short of an embarrassment. One of the reasons for this is that the average *shule* puts all of their resources into the upkeep of the unnecessary, and hardly ever used, mammoth cathedral-like building, rather than into catering and great programming.

4. At least once a month, the community should hold a communal meal, either for Friday night dinner or Shabbos lunch, to which the entire community is invited. Shalom Aleichem should be sung together and special entertainments for children provided. This affords an opportunity for the community to come together as a family and bond well beyond the pleasantries that are offered as people depart the *shule*. A guest speaker could be invited as a draw on these occasions in order to offer new ideas to the congregation and stimulate further discussion. A member of the community – either male or female – should also be asked to deliver a *dvar Torah*, a prepared insight into the weekly Bible reading, and everyone present should get up and offer a short, yet meaningful, L'Chaim for the coming week.

5. The basic structure of the Jewish community ought to change. There should be a devolution from the centralised institutions in favour of independent congregations which empower the rabbi and his board to implement new ideas without pressure for conformity from the centre. I immediately see the indispensable need for a Chief Rabbi, who serves as the spokesman and leader of the community. And there can be none better in that post than our current, im-

mensely eloquent, Chief Rabbi, Dr Jonathan Sacks. But the United Synagogue, in its current form, has outlived its purpose.

The same is true of the other central offices of Masorti and Reform. This is the age, not of the corporation, but rather of the entrepreneur and the individual. The strong centralisation of the Jewish community is sapping the entrepreneurial spirit out of its rabbis. They are facing an uphill struggle, attempting against the odds to bring in disaffected and bored constituents. In these circumstances rabbis can ill afford being straight-jacketed by a central office which, through no fault of its officers, cannot understand the needs of each individual communities. We must begin to trust the generals in the field. American Jewry, for example, is infinitely more creative than Anglo-Jewry, and this can be attributed in no small measure to the lack of any centralising authority that forces rabbis to conform. What should replace the United Synagogue is a far more loosely constructed federation which cooperate, but do not have power over an individual rabbi's programmes.

6. The roles of today's rabbis ought to be redefined. Rabbis must be trained and expected to be teachers and communal directors, much more than pastors. Certainly, the pastoral roles of visiting the sick, conducting funerals, and doing stone-settings, are highly important. But they do not come near the importance of setting up lectures, seminars, classes, debates, social events, and anything else that will bring existing and new members enthusiastically through the *shule* door. A rabbi's pastoral role is aimed principally at the older segments of the community. But this needs to be rebalanced. We need to restructure his role so that the majority of his time

is spent educating and inspiring the young. The success of a rabbi should not be measured by the eloquence of his sermon, but rather by the number of people he attracts to the synagogue. Rabbis must be expected to stage exciting and regular *shule* events, and spend most of their time teaching and imparting the beauty of Jewish wisdom and learning to an uneducated community who are cynical about the relevance of Torah to the modern age.

7. Women ought to be allowed to take leading roles in structuring and inspiring communities. They should be invited to serve as presidents of synagogues. Although orthodox Judaism does not allow female rabbis, women are of course permitted to be teachers and experts in the Torah. Twice a month, a woman should offer a *dvar* Torah at the *kiddush* following the services, attended by the entire congregation.

8. I believe in the power and truth of orthodoxy and in the Torah's ability to win arguments in the marketplace of ideas. But we are all one people and both Orthodoxy and Reform should, therefore, have twice monthly public seminars on religious issues, aimed at healing the rift which divides them, so that any disagreements which do arise will at least be substantive disagreements rather than the embarrassing, trivial nonsense that currently divides us. Disputes as to whether or not the Torah is entirely divine or whether man is empowered to change religious tenets are a whole lot better than arguments about who was or was not present at a funeral, or reading someone's private correspondence. The discussion and debate of real issues will finally pull us out of tabloid Judaism in whose mire we all find ourselves today.

Greatness beckons at the doors of any dormant community like Anglo Jewry, if only we can finally muster the courage to invite her in.

References

Paul Johnson, *History of the Jews* (1988)

Elie Wiesel, *The Town Beyond the Wall* (1964)

Norman Lamm, *Faith and Doubt: Studies in Traditional Jewish Thought* (1964)

Robert Lee, *Religion and Leisure in America* (1963)

Victor Frankl, *Man's Search for Meaning* (1964)

Sigmund Freud, *Totem and Taboo* (1913)

James Paterson and Peter Kin, *The Day America Told the Truth* (1990)

Charles Darwin, *The Origin of Species by Natural Selection: The Preservation of Favoured Races in the Struggle for Life* (1863)

Robert Wright, *The Moral Animal: Why We Are the Way We Are: The New Science of Evolutionary Psychology* (1994)

Baruch Spinoza, *Theologico-Political Treatise* (1670)

Jean-Paul Sartre, *Anti-Semite and Jew* (1995)

Alan Dershowitz, *The Vanishing American Jew: In Search of Jewish Identity for the Twenty-First Century* (1997)

Joseph Soloveitchik, *The Lonely Man of Faith* (1965)

H.S. Chamberlain, *Foundations of the Nineteenth Century* (1899)

Index